'THE COTS\

BOOK 3 — THE SOUTH AND WE!

This guide book, which is one of a ‹
area, contains exact, but simple directic
visits to such well known places as Cirenc
Painswick, Prinknash, Chedworth Ror.   ....ne Dutisbournes, with an
exploration of the quiet villages that lie hidden beyond the network of busy main roads.
The 'Main Circle' Route (Maps 1 – 10) shown on the Key Map opposite, covers 110 miles, and is far too long for a leisurely day's journey. We have therefore included 'link routes' to break this up into several smaller circles. Each route, being circular, may of course be started at any point suitable to you. At various points it is possible to link on to the other 'Cotswold by Car' books, and certain places are of necessity to be found in more than one book. We have however kept this practice to a minimum, and each book is almost wholly complementary to its fellows.

HOW TO USE YOUR BOOK ON THE ROUTE

Each double page makes up a complete picture of the country ahead of you. On the left you will find a one inch to the mile strip map, with the route marked by a series of dashes. Direction is always from top to bottom, so that the map may be looked at in conjunction with the 'directions to the driver', with which it is cross referenced by a letter itemising each junction point. This enables the driver to have exact guidance every time an opportunity for changing direction occurs, even if it is only "Keep straight, not left!"

With mileage intervals shown, the driver should even have warning when to expect those 'moments of decision', and if a sign post exists we have used this to help you with 'Follow sign marked . . .' column. However re-signing is always in progress, and this may lead to slight differences in sign marking in some cases . . . So beware of freshly erected signs.

We have also included a description of the towns and villages through which you will pass, together with some photographs to illustrate the route.

Much of the area covered in this volume is not as well known as the classic 'North Cotswolds' of Broadway, Chipping Campden, Stow and Bourton. However it contains equally beautiful countryside, and its towns and villages deserve to be better known and more widely appreciated. Here are deep valleys where the clothiers made their fortunes, and spent so wisely upon the construction of fine churches and exquisite manors and town houses. Here is dramatic edge country with splendid views out over the Severn estuary; and rolling wolds with broad prospects to the Wiltshire Downs. Here are great parks with splendid mansions, small Norman churches, great hill forts and fascinating Roman villas.

To gain full enjoyment from these journeys, be prepared to leave your car as often as possible. This will give you the opportunity to engage in such activities as strolling down village streets, learning over bridge parapets to gaze into the clear streams below, or simply relaxing in some of England's most tranquil countryside.

When your journey is complete, you will have begun to understand the unique charm of the Cotswolds. However, the hundreds of turnings that you have previously had to ignore, will we hope, tempt you to return again to discover more of the quiet roads and villages, that await you among the wolds.

COMPILED BY PETER AND HELEN TITCHMARSH
PHOTOGRAPHY BY ALAN AND PETER TITCHMARSH

MAP 1

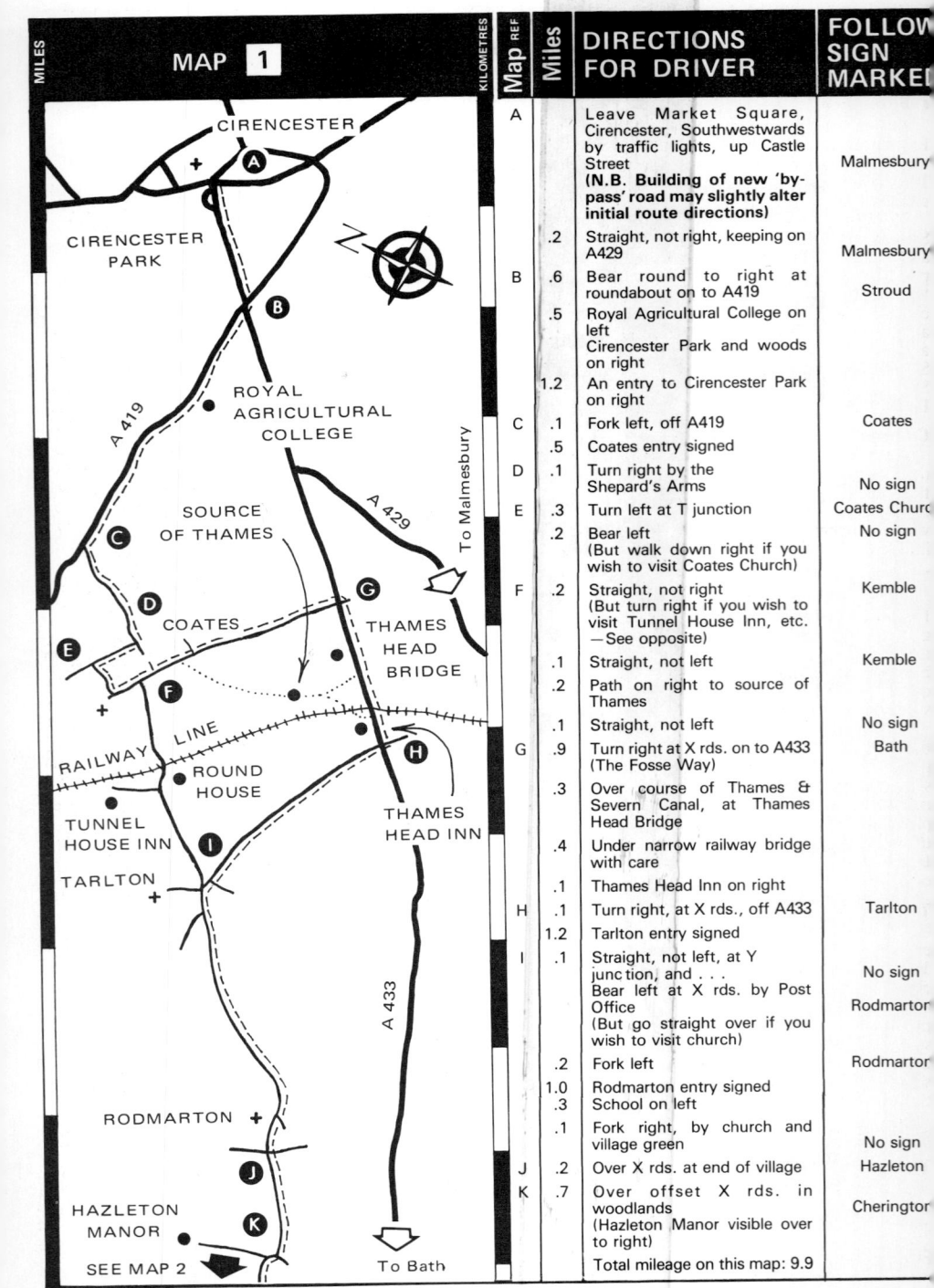

DIRECTIONS FOR DRIVER / FOLLOW SIGN MARKED

Map Ref	Miles	Directions for Driver	Follow Sign Marked
A		Leave Market Square, Cirencester, Southwestwards by traffic lights, up Castle Street (N.B. Building of new 'by-pass' road may slightly alter initial route directions)	Malmesbury
	.2	Straight, not right, keeping on A429	Malmesbury
B	.6	Bear round to right at roundabout on to A419	Stroud
	.5	Royal Agricultural College on left Cirencester Park and woods on right	
	1.2	An entry to Cirencester Park on right	
C	.1	Fork left, off A419	Coates
	.5	Coates entry signed	
D	.1	Turn right by the Shepard's Arms	No sign
E	.3	Turn left at T junction	Coates Church
	.2	Bear left (But walk down right if you wish to visit Coates Church)	No sign
F	.2	Straight, not right (But turn right if you wish to visit Tunnel House Inn, etc. — See opposite)	Kemble
	.1	Straight, not left	Kemble
	.2	Path on right to source of Thames	
	.1	Straight, not left	No sign
G	.9	Turn right at X rds. on to A433 (The Fosse Way)	Bath
	.3	Over course of Thames & Severn Canal, at Thames Head Bridge	
	.4	Under narrow railway bridge with care	
	.1	Thames Head Inn on right	
H	.1	Turn right, at X rds., off A433	Tarlton
	1.2	Tarlton entry signed	
I	.1	Straight, not left, at Y junction, and . . .	No sign
		Bear left at X rds. by Post Office (But go straight over if you wish to visit church)	Rodmarton
	.2	Fork left	Rodmarton
	1.0	Rodmarton entry signed	
	.3	School on left	
	.1	Fork right, by church and village green	No sign
J	.2	Over X rds. at end of village	Hazleton
K	.7	Over offset X rds. in woodlands (Hazleton Manor visible over to right)	Cherington
		Total mileage on this map: 9.9	

CROWN COPYRIGHT RESERVED

PLACES OF INTEREST ON THE ROUTE

Cirencester
Busy market town, standing on the site of Corinium, Roman Britain's second largest city. Meeting point of the Fosse Way, Ermin Street and Akeman Street over 1800 years ago, Cirencester still thrives today as the centre of life in the southern Cotswolds.

Many of the gaily coloured shops in the Market Square retain their individuality and charm, and over all presides the magnificent Perpendicular tower and porch of the Parish Church. This fine 15th century 'wool church' has a splendid roof illuminated by clerestory windows, medieval stained glass in the east and west windows, a painted 'wineglass' pulpit, and also many fine brasses. See also the surviving arcade of St. John's Hospital (founded by Henry II) in Spitalgate Street, and the really excellent Corinium Museum in Park Street. (For Cirencester Park, see page 23.)

1. Cirencester Church

Coates
A small village on the high wolds with a neat Perpendicular towered church, in company with a rectory and farmhouse . . . two most beautiful houses. Passing from the tidy churchyard, through a Norman doorway, we were delighted with the simplicity of the church's interior.

Thames and Severn Canal (a diversion)
This was opened in 1789, (not a very auspicious year for such an aristocratic enterprise) and finally abandoned in 1927. Its closure was one of the greatest tragedies of English canal history, for if it had only been kept open until today, it would have provided an outstandingly beautiful link between our two great river systems.

We first pass one of the fascinating 'round houses' . . . little Gothic towers, built at intervals for the canal maintenance men. Then turn right by the inn sign, and drive beside the canal 'ditch', here shaded by massive beech trees, to the Tunnel House Inn, a pleasant 18th century building close to the entrance to the canal tunnel. This entrance is still embellished with Doric columns and niches, and marked the beginning of a 2¼ mile tunnel to Sapperton (see page 23).

2. Canal Round House near Coates

3. Tunnel House Inn Sign

Thames Head
It is a fine walk across the fields to Trewsbury Mead, either from our road beyond Point F, or from the Thames Head Inn. However be prepared for an anti-climax, for you will probably find nothing more than a muddy depression beneath a tree, with a granite slab proclaiming this to be the source of the Thames. This stone replaces a handsome statue of Neptune which has been removed to St. John's Lock below Lechlade, as it sadly became the subject of vandalism within a short time of its arrival here in 1958.

Do not overlook the 'earthworks' of the Thames & Severn Canal, which used to run close by.

4. The Tunnel House Inn

Tarlton
Pleasantly scattered little village with a pretty, creeper covered Post Office. The small 'Norman' church was re-built in 1875, and is not of great interest.

5. Rodmarton Church

Rodmarton (see page 5)

MAP 2

Map REF	Miles	DIRECTIONS FOR DRIVER	FOLLOW SIGN MARKED
		Pass pleasant woodlands	
A	1.0	Bear right at T junction	No sign
	.9	Cherington entry signed	
		Straight, not right	No sign
	.2	Turn right by village green (But bear left if you wish to visit church)	Avening
B	.1	Fork left on hill	Avening
	.1	Pleasant wooded valley below us to right	
	.1	Now dropping steeply down	
C	.4	Straight, not right in Nag's Head hamlet (House on right, used to be The Nag's Head Inn) (WE ARE JOINED HERE FROM THE END OF MAP 14)	No sign
	.3	Straight, not left (Avening Court down left)	No sign
D	.2	Bear left, with care, on to wider road, and . . . Enter Avening	Avening
	.1	Over small X rds. by bus shelter	No sign
E	.1	Bear half left, on to B4014 by the Cross Inn (But go straight over if you wish to visit church .3)	Tetbury
	.3	Straight, not right, keeping on B4014	No sign
F	1.1	Turn right, at X rds., off B4014	Chavenage
G	.6	Turn left at T junction	No sign
		Pleasant tree lined road	
	.2	Keep left, by gate pillars (It is possible to walk down right to visit Chavenage church, but not recommended)	No sign
	.1	Chavenage House on right	
H	.7	Bear right at Y junction	No sign
I	.1	Bear up right at T junction	No sign
J	.7	Over X rds., crossing A4135 (BUT TURN RIGHT IF YOU WISH TO START MAP 15) (But turn left if you wish to visit Tetbury—.8 to centre)	Westonbirt
K	1.4	Fork left by cottages and farm	Westonbirt
		Total mileage on this map: 8.7	

IN FROM MAP 14
CHERINGTON
NAG'S HEAD
AVENING COURT
AVENING
B 4014
To Tetbury
CHAVENAGE
A 4135
SEE MAP 15
To Dursley
SEE MAP 3

CROWN COPYRIGHT RESERVED

PLACES OF INTEREST ON THE ROUTE

Rodmarton (see page 2)
This has a small green overlooked by quiet cottages, and an attractively spired church. Pollarded trees create a 'lych-gate' effect over the churchyard gate, and there are several pleasant tombs in the churchyard. Unfortunately the interior was ruthlessly scraped by the Victorians, but there are old stone floors, several handsome 18th and 19th century monuments, and a 15th century brass of a lawyer complete with his cap and gown.

Cherington
The unspoilt Yew Tree Inn and several dignified 18th century cottages overlook a large green, which is endowed with a Victorian drinking fountain inscribed 'Let Him that is athirst, come'. The church has a Norman south doorway with tympanum, and an Early English chancel (unfortunately scraped). We particularly liked the pulpit incorporating carved Flemish (?) panels, and the handsome Renaissance candle-holder beside it.

Nag's Head
Delicious little hamlet taking its name from an inn of that name, now a private house. It has a row of small houses looking southwards over a quiet valley . . . everyone's dream for retirement.

Avening
Large village in a valley, with pleasant old shops and houses, and several inns. The early Norman cruciform church is well sited in a steep sloping churchyard. Its Norman north doorway has been filled in with a smaller Perpendicular one, and there is a Norman chancel arch, a vaulted tower crossing, and a vaulted chancel. Behind the organ, in the south transept, there is a small 'museum' including a model of Avening Long Barrow, and models of the church at various stages of its long life. Do not miss the two unusually pleasant windows in the nave.

Chavenage
Our view from the road provides a mouth-watering impression of this fine 16th century manor house. It is possible to walk behind, through its yards (see Route Directions) to the little church . . . Medieval tower, figures from a 17th century tomb cemented into the porch . . . otherwise little of interest, and rather an anti-climax after our view of the house from the road.

Tetbury
Small market town, and antiques centre, on the busy A433. Its 17th century Market House, on three rows of delightfully dumpy pillars, was used for wool trading, and there are many handsome 17th and 18th century houses in Tetbury that bear witness to its prosperity as a wool collecting centre for the cloth towns and villages to its north and west. The elegant 18th century Gothic church, with its beautifully proportioned interior should on no account be missed.

1. The Green at Cherington

2. Nag's Head Hamlet

3. Chavenage

4. Market House, Tetbury

MAP 3

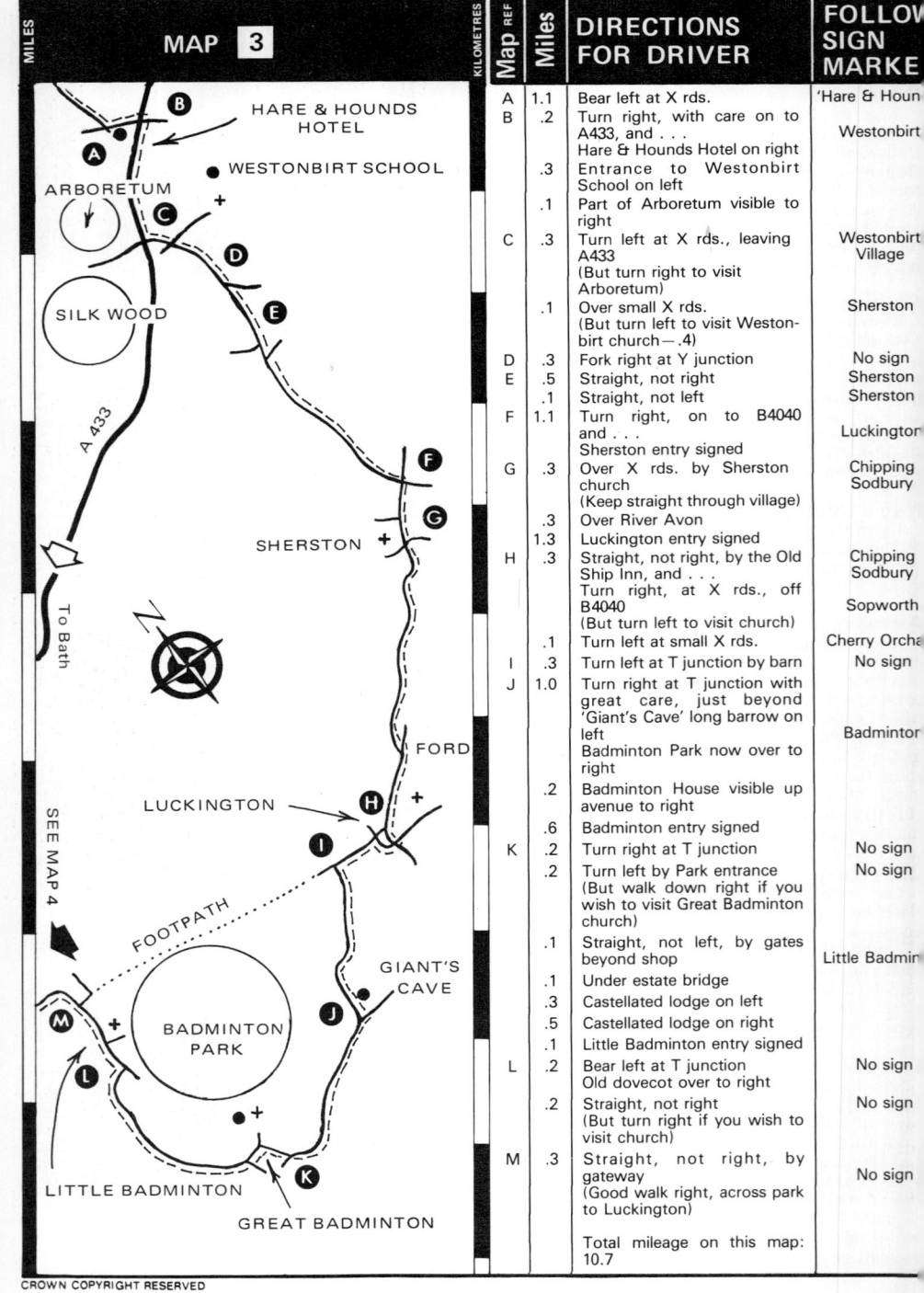

Locations on map: HARE & HOUNDS HOTEL, WESTONBIRT SCHOOL, ARBORETUM, SILK WOOD, SHERSTON, FORD, LUCKINGTON, FOOTPATH, GIANT'S CAVE, BADMINTON PARK, LITTLE BADMINTON, GREAT BADMINTON. A433 to Bath. SEE MAP 4.

Map Ref	Miles	DIRECTIONS FOR DRIVER	FOLLOW SIGN MARKED
A	1.1	Bear left at X rds.	'Hare & Houn
B	.2	Turn right, with care on to A433, and . . . Hare & Hounds Hotel on right	Westonbirt
	.3	Entrance to Westonbirt School on left	
	.1	Part of Arboretum visible to right	
C	.3	Turn left at X rds., leaving A433 (But turn right to visit Arboretum)	Westonbirt Village
	.1	Over small X rds. (But turn left to visit Westonbirt church—.4)	Sherston
D	.3	Fork right at Y junction	No sign
E	.5	Straight, not right	Sherston
	.1	Straight, not left	Sherston
F	1.1	Turn right, on to B4040 and . . . Sherston entry signed	Luckington
G	.3	Over X rds. by Sherston church (Keep straight through village)	Chipping Sodbury
	.3	Over River Avon	
	1.3	Luckington entry signed	
H	.3	Straight, not right, by the Old Ship Inn, and . . .	Chipping Sodbury
		Turn right, at X rds., off B4040 (But turn left to visit church)	Sopworth
	.1	Turn left at small X rds.	Cherry Orcha
I	.3	Turn left at T junction by barn	No sign
J	1.0	Turn right at T junction with great care, just beyond 'Giant's Cave' long barrow on left Badminton Park now over to right	Badminton
	.2	Badminton House visible up avenue to right	
	.6	Badminton entry signed	
K	.2	Turn right at T junction	No sign
	.2	Turn left by Park entrance (But walk down right if you wish to visit Great Badminton church)	No sign
	.1	Straight, not left, by gates beyond shop	Little Badmin
	.1	Under estate bridge	
	.3	Castellated lodge on left	
	.5	Castellated lodge on right	
	.1	Little Badminton entry signed	
L	.2	Bear left at T junction Old dovecot over to right	No sign
	.2	Straight, not right (But turn right if you wish to visit church)	No sign
M	.3	Straight, not right, by gateway (Good walk right, across park to Luckington)	No sign

Total mileage on this map: 10.7

CROWN COPYRIGHT RESERVED

6

PLACES OF INTEREST ON THE ROUTE

Westonbirt
The magnificent mansion was built for R. S. Holford by Lewis Vulliamy (1863 – 70), and is now a girls' school. The present village was also built by Vulliamy, but the rows of cottages have mellowed delightfully. The church, at the very end of the village, is overlooked by the great mansion, and apart from its tower, has been so completely restored, as to be almost wholly Victorian in feeling.

Westonbirt Arboretum
This world famous collection of trees was started by R. S. Holford, the owner of Westonbirt, as early as 1829. It now covers 116 acres, and is managed by the Forestry Commission. Here is a vast variety of trees in carefully contrived harmony, with rhododendrons, azaleas and camelias in profusion. Come here in late October when the various maples are almost on fire with colour.

Sherston
A large village with wide main street. It lies only a mile or two over the boundary into Wiltshire, but it already has a slightly 'West Country', rather than Cotswold, flavour. It has a fine church, with stout tower surprisingly built as late as 1730, and a handsomely vaulted Perpendicular porch. There are several interesting 18th and 19th century monuments inside, although a Victorian atmosphere prevails.

Luckington
Has a minute lock-up, and a small church with 13th century origins tucked away at the end of the village beside a fine Queen Anne house, Luckington Court.

The Giant's Cave
A Stone Age long barrow (about 2000 BC) beneath a clump of trees to the left of our road at Point J. ON PRIVATE LAND.

Great Badminton
Delightful estate village with houses and cottages of the 17th, 18th and 19th centuries. The church, built in 1785 is attached to the mansion (see below), and contains a splendid series of monuments to the Dukes of Beaufort.

Badminton House
Large mansion dating from the latter half of the 17th century, when the Somerset family had to abandon Raglan Castle. (The Third Marquess was created the First Duke of Beaufort in 1682.) William Kent embellished it in the 18th century and built the lovely Worcester Lodge at the north end of the park (view from A433, west of Didmarton). The game of badminton was invented here, the standard measurements being dictated by the dimensions of its hall. However Badminton is now best known for its 'Three Day Event' horse trials, held in the magnificent park each spring.

Little Badminton
A small village scattered in fields to the north-east of the park, with a pretty dovecot, and a very small church in a neat churchyard.

1. Westonbirt Arboretum

2. Westonbirt Church

3. Sherston Tower

4. Sherston Porch

5. Badminton

6. Dovecot, Little Badminton

MAP 4

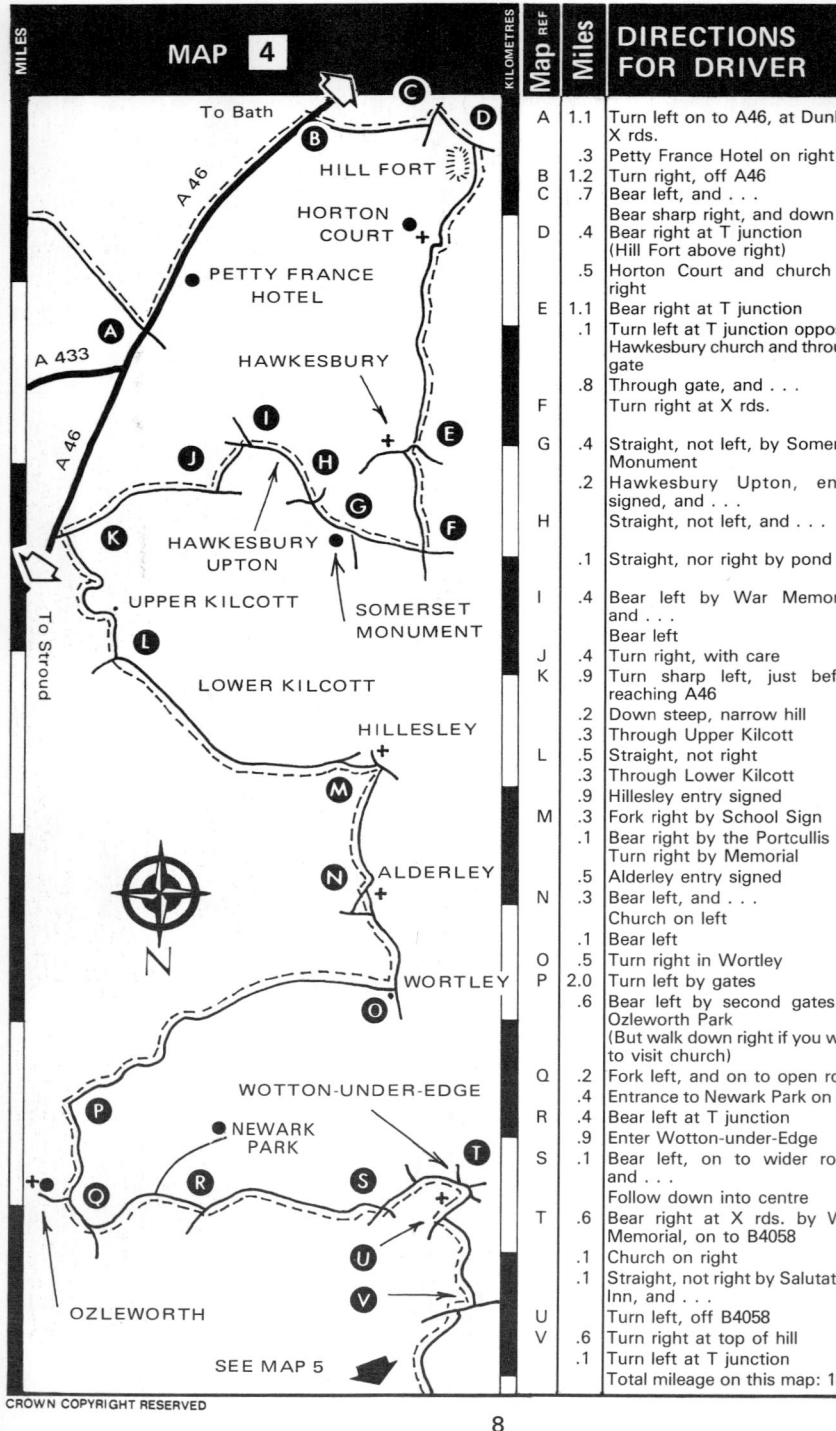

Map REF	Miles	DIRECTIONS FOR DRIVER	FOLLOW SIGN MARKED
A	1.1	Turn left on to A46, at Dunkirk X rds.	Bath
	.3	Petty France Hotel on right	
B	1.2	Turn right, off A46	Horton
C	.7	Bear left, and . . .	Horton
		Bear sharp right, and down hill	Horton
D	.4	Bear right at T junction (Hill Fort above right)	Hawkesbury
	.5	Horton Court and church on right	
E	1.1	Bear right at T junction	No sign
	.1	Turn left at T junction opposite Hawkesbury church and through gate	No sign
	.8	Through gate, and . . .	
F		Turn right at X rds.	Hawkesbury Upton
G	.4	Straight, not left, by Somerset Monument	Dunkirk
	.2	Hawkesbury Upton, entry signed, and . . .	
H		Straight, not left, and . . .	Hawkesbury Upton
	.1	Straight, nor right by pond	Hawkesbury Upton
I	.4	Bear left by War Memorial, and . . .	Starveall
		Bear left	'Back Street'
J	.4	Turn right, with care	No sign
K	.9	Turn sharp left, just before reaching A46	Kilcott
	.2	Down steep, narrow hill	
	.3	Through Upper Kilcott	
L	.5	Straight, not right	No sign
	.3	Through Lower Kilcott	
	.9	Hillesley entry signed	
M	.3	Fork right by School Sign	No sign
	.1	Bear right by the Portcullis Inn	Kingswood
		Turn right by Memorial	Alderley
	.5	Alderley entry signed	
N	.3	Bear left, and . . .	Wotton
		Church on left	
	.1	Bear left	Wortley
O	.5	Turn right in Wortley	Ozleworth
P	2.0	Turn left by gates	No sign
	.6	Bear left by second gates to Ozleworth Park (But walk down right if you wish to visit church)	No sign
Q	.2	Fork left, and on to open road	'Gates'
	.4	Entrance to Newark Park on left	
R	.4	Bear left at T junction	No sign
	.9	Enter Wotton-under-Edge	
S	.1	Bear left, on to wider road, and . . .	No sign
		Follow down into centre	
T	.6	Bear right at X rds. by War Memorial, on to B4058	Nailsworth
	.1	Church on right	
	.1	Straight, not right by Salutation Inn, and . . .	No sign
U		Turn left, off B4058	'Adey's Lane'
V	.6	Turn right at top of hill	No sign
	.1	Turn left at T junction	Waterley Bottom
		Total mileage on this map: 18.7	

CROWN COPYRIGHT RESERVED

PLACES OF INTEREST ON THE ROUTE

Horton
Lies beneath an Iron Age promontory fort (at Point D), with its church about half a mile beyond. This is set beneath the wooded Cotswold edge, beside Horton Court, a lovely manor house, with a Norman hall and a detached 16th century ambulatory. The church has a well proportioned Perpendicular tower and a vaulted porch of the same period. In the pleasantly white painted interior there is a Jacobean pulpit, and two handsome 18th century wall tablets.

Hawkesbury
The tall towered, mainly Perpendicular church stands almost alone, where a wooded valley opens out from the hilly edge. It all looks splendid from the outside, but once through the Norman north doorway, one is greeted with a brutally scraped interior. However, stop to look at the 15th century stone pulpit, and the monuments to the Jenkinson family (one of whom, the Second Earl of Liverpool, was Prime Minister at the time of Waterloo).

The Somerset Monument
High stone tower with a slightly oriental flavour, built by Lewis Vulliamy in 1846, and commemorating General Lord Robert Somerset. At least six counties may be seen from the top of this formidable landmark . . . well worth the considerable effort.

Upper and Lower Kilcott
Two quiet little hamlets tucked away in the edge country. Lower Kilcott has a small 18th century water mill with some of its machinery still intact. NOT OPEN TO THE PUBLIC.

Hillesley (or Hillsley)
Modest village endowed with a severe little Baptist chapel, two inns, the Portcullis and the Fleece, and an ambitious Victorian church.

Alderley
Rosehill, next to the church, was built by the industrious Vulliamy in 1860, but there are several earlier houses in this small village. The church, apart from its Perpendicular tower, was re-built in 1802, and has an elegant white painted interior, with a series of stylish monuments, one of which is by the celebrated Sir Francis Chantrey.

Ozleworth
Walk up the short drive to handsome 18th century Ozleworth Park (house), and round behind it to visit the Norman church, with its very rare hexagonal tower.

Newark Park
Elizabethan Hunting Lodge built by the Poyntz family on the edge of a cliff, and converted into a castellated house by James Wyatt in 1790.

Wotton-under-Edge
Attractive little town which still shows signs of its prosperity in the 17th and 18th century cloth trade. The church has a fine Perpendicular tower and a large over restored interior. Do not miss the splendid late 14th century brasses of Lord and Lady Berkeley. Glass fibre copy usually on display.)

1. Mill at Lower Kilcott

2. In Ozleworth Bottom

3. Wotton-under-Edge

4. South Porch, Wotton-under-Edge

MAP 5

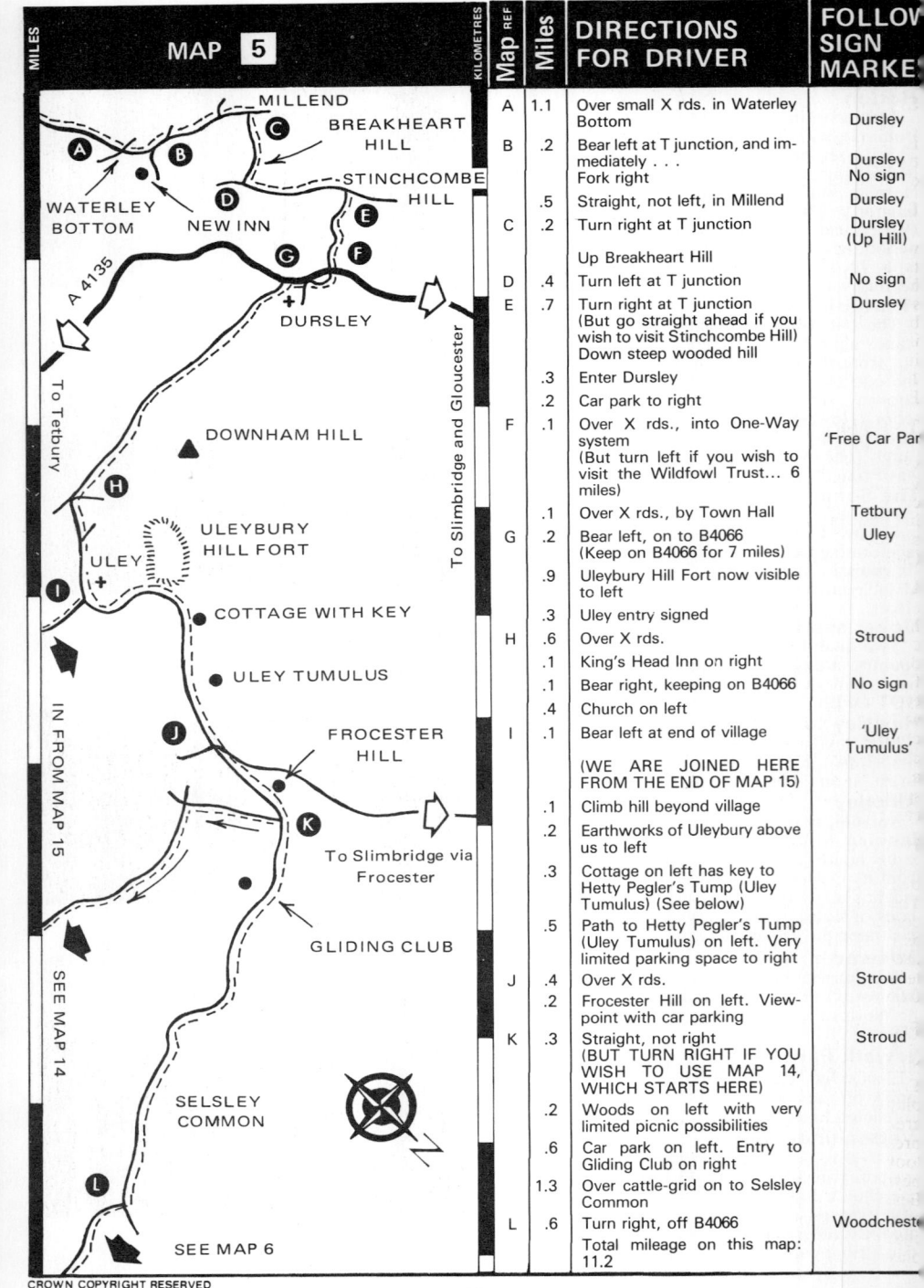

Map showing locations: MILLEND, BREAKHEART HILL, STINCHCOMBE HILL, WATERLEY BOTTOM, NEW INN, DURSLEY, DOWNHAM HILL, ULEYBURY HILL FORT, ULEY, COTTAGE WITH KEY, ULEY TUMULUS, FROCESTER HILL, GLIDING CLUB, SELSLEY COMMON. Roads: A4135, To Tetbury, To Slimbridge and Gloucester, To Slimbridge via Frocester, IN FROM MAP 15, SEE MAP 14, SEE MAP 6.

Map Ref	Miles	DIRECTIONS FOR DRIVER	FOLLOW SIGN MARKED
A	1.1	Over small X rds. in Waterley Bottom	Dursley
B	.2	Bear left at T junction, and immediately . . . Fork right	Dursley No sign
	.5	Straight, not left, in Millend	Dursley
C	.2	Turn right at T junction Up Breakheart Hill	Dursley (Up Hill)
D	.4	Turn left at T junction	No sign
E	.7	Turn right at T junction (But go straight ahead if you wish to visit Stinchcombe Hill) Down steep wooded hill	Dursley
	.3	Enter Dursley	
	.2	Car park to right	
F	.1	Over X rds., into One-Way system (But turn left if you wish to visit the Wildfowl Trust... 6 miles)	'Free Car Park'
	.1	Over X rds., by Town Hall	Tetbury
G	.2	Bear left, on to B4066 (Keep on B4066 for 7 miles)	Uley
	.9	Uleybury Hill Fort now visible to left	
	.3	Uley entry signed	
H	.6	Over X rds.	Stroud
	.1	King's Head Inn on right	
	.1	Bear right, keeping on B4066	No sign
	.4	Church on left	
I	.1	Bear left at end of village	'Uley Tumulus'
		(WE ARE JOINED HERE FROM THE END OF MAP 15)	
	.1	Climb hill beyond village	
	.2	Earthworks of Uleybury above us to left	
	.3	Cottage on left has key to Hetty Pegler's Tump (Uley Tumulus) (See below)	
	.5	Path to Hetty Pegler's Tump (Uley Tumulus) on left. Very limited parking space to right	
J	.4	Over X rds.	Stroud
	.2	Frocester Hill on left. Viewpoint with car parking	
K	.3	Straight, not right (BUT TURN RIGHT IF YOU WISH TO USE MAP 14, WHICH STARTS HERE)	Stroud
	.2	Woods on left with very limited picnic possibilities	
	.6	Car park on left. Entry to Gliding Club on right	
	1.3	Over cattle-grid on to Selsley Common	
L	.6	Turn right, off B4066 Total mileage on this map: 11.7	Woodchester

CROWN COPYRIGHT RESERVED

10

PLACES OF INTEREST ON THE ROUTE

Stinchcombe Hill
Part of this area is used as a golf course, but there is parking space for cars, good walking opportunities and fine views out over the Berkeley Vale, especially from Drakestone Point.

Dursley
Busy market town beneath the Cotswold edge, with extensive industry replacing the vanished cloth trade. It is centred upon a delightful 18th century Market House/Town Hall, complete with elegant statue of Queen Anne. The nearby church has a beautifully vaulted Perpendicular porch, but its interior has been disappointingly over-restored. The impressive tower was re-built in the Gothic style in 1709, and is only twenty years older than the Town Hall.

The Wildfowl Trust, Slimbridge
This diversion from Dursley, on A4135, and then via Moorend or Cambridge, and through Slimbridge village, takes us to the largest and most varied collection of waterfowl in the world. Go if possible in winter if you wish to see the wild geese on the shores of the estuary from observation towers. (Regret no space for detailed directions.)

Uley
Large village with many delightful 18th century houses . . . evidence of Uley's prosperity as a cloth centre until the Industrial Revolution, when industrial production shifted from weaver's cottage to factory loom. Do not miss the King's Head, a typically handsome 18th century building complete with brightly painted George 1st sign. The Victorian church is well sited above the road, and beside the churchyard there is a path leading up to Uleybury, an extensive Iron Age hill fort, which provides a splendid walk on a wide grassy terrace around its ramparts.

Hetty Pegler's Tump (or Uley Tumulus)
A Stone Age chambered long barrow . . . the burial place of at least 28 of our distant ancestors. The eastern end can be explored, but unless you come here after a long dry spell, bring old clothing, as it can be a wet and muddy experience. The very low entrance is kept locked, but the key may be collected from the cottage at the top of the hill beyond Uley (see Route Directions). Take a good torch.

Frocester Hill
A lovely open place, which is owned by the National Trust, but leased to the Gloucestershire Trust for Nature Conservation (see the coloured plaques depicting various aspects of nature in the area). There is a topograph, or viewing table, presented by the A.A., and on a clear day, one can look out across the Severn estuary, and the low hills beyond, to the Black Mountains and the Brecon Beacons. Gliders from the nearby club further enrich the scene with colourful movement and enchanting wind noise as they drift overhead like playful seagulls.

1. On Breakheart Hill

2. Town Hall, Dursley

3. House at Uley

4. On Frocester Hill

MAP 6

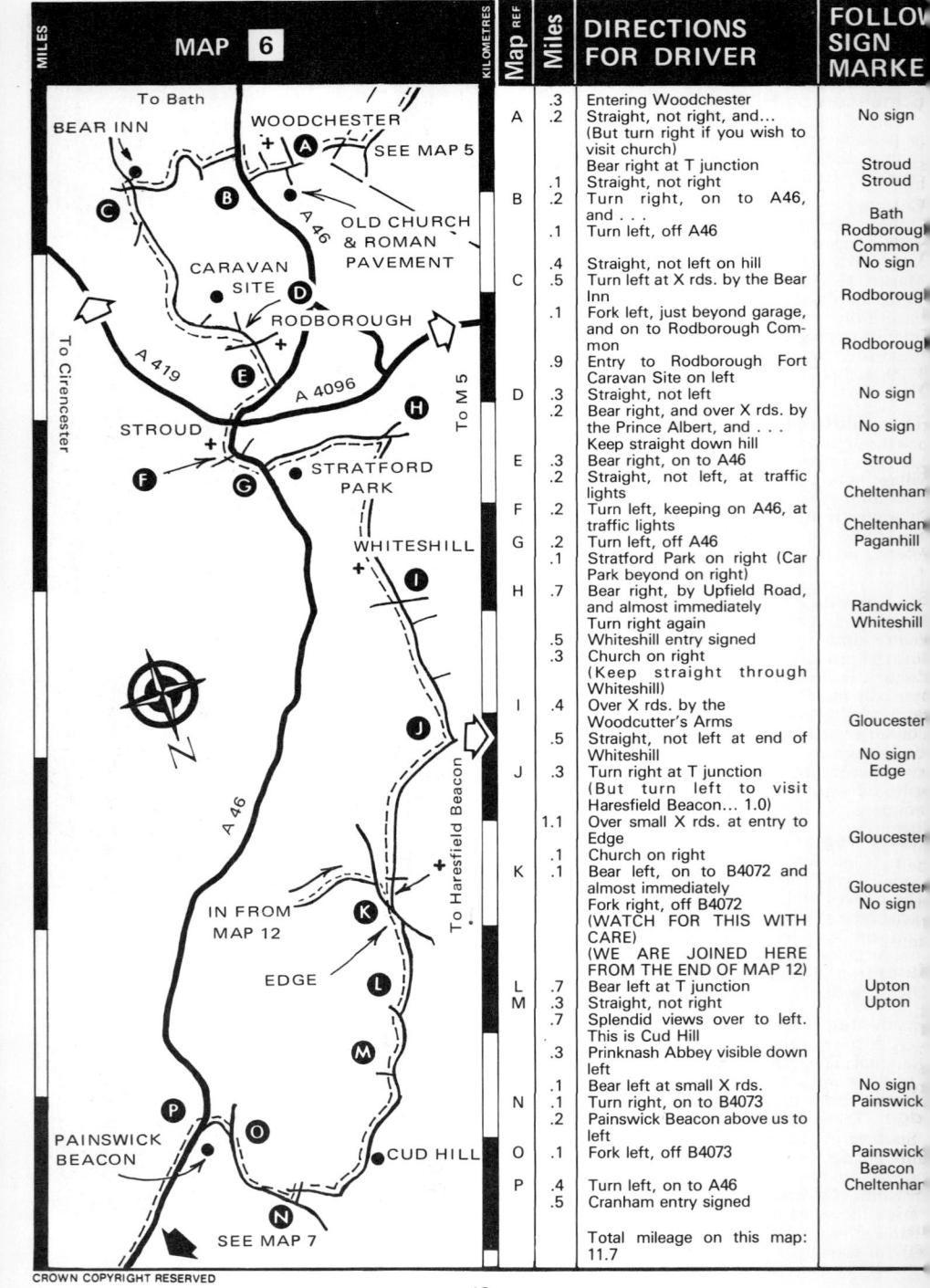

Map REF	Miles	DIRECTIONS FOR DRIVER	FOLLOW SIGN MARKED
A	.3	Entering Woodchester	
	.2	Straight, not right, and... (But turn right if you wish to visit church)	No sign
		Bear right at T junction	Stroud
	.1	Straight, not right	Stroud
B	.2	Turn right, on to A46, and . . .	Bath
	.1	Turn left, off A46	Rodborough Common
	.4	Straight, not left on hill	No sign
C	.5	Turn left at X rds. by the Bear Inn	Rodborough
	.1	Fork left, just beyond garage, and on to Rodborough Common	Rodborough
	.9	Entry to Rodborough Fort Caravan Site on left	
D	.3	Straight, not left	No sign
	.2	Bear right, and over X rds. by the Prince Albert, and . . .	No sign
		Keep straight down hill	
E	.3	Bear right, on to A46	Stroud
	.2	Straight, not left, at traffic lights	Cheltenham
F	.2	Turn left, keeping on A46, at traffic lights	Cheltenham
G	.2	Turn left, off A46	Paganhill
	.1	Stratford Park on right (Car Park beyond on right)	
H	.7	Bear right, by Upfield Road, and almost immediately	Randwick
		Turn right again	Whiteshill
	.5	Whiteshill entry signed	
	.3	Church on right (Keep straight through Whiteshill)	
I	.4	Over X rds. by the Woodcutter's Arms	Gloucester
	.5	Straight, not left at end of Whiteshill	No sign
J	.3	Turn right at T junction (But turn left to visit Haresfield Beacon... 1.0)	Edge
	1.1	Over small X rds. at entry to Edge	Gloucester
	.1	Church on right	
K	.1	Bear left, on to B4072 and almost immediately	Gloucester
		Fork right, off B4072 (WATCH FOR THIS WITH CARE) (WE ARE JOINED HERE FROM THE END OF MAP 12)	No sign
L	.7	Bear left at T junction	Upton
M	.3	Straight, not right	Upton
	.7	Splendid views over to left. This is Cud Hill	
	.3	Prinknash Abbey visible down left	
	.1	Bear left at small X rds.	No sign
N	.5	Turn right, on to B4073	Painswick
	.2	Painswick Beacon above us to left	
O	.1	Fork left, off B4073	Painswick Beacon
P	.4	Turn left, on to A46	Cheltenham
	.5	Cranham entry signed	
		Total mileage on this map: 11.7	

PLACES OF INTEREST ON THE ROUTE

Woodchester

This sits on the steep western slopes of the Avon valley, linking Stroud and Nailsworth, and there are several 18th and 19th century mills in the valley bottom. The Victorian church contains a few monuments taken from the old church, but it is the churchyard where the older building stood, that contains Woodchester's great treasure . . . THE WOODCHESTER ROMAN PAVEMENT.

This is a splendid mosaic pavement, part of a large Roman villa, first systematically excavated in 1796. It usually lies buried in the old churchyard, but in recent times it has usually been uncovered for one summer every ten years (possibly next in 1993). This is one of the finest Roman mosaics outside the Mediterranean area, and it is a pity that it cannot be roofed over and put on permanent display. A good replica of it was made some years ago, but at the time of writing, it is in store awaiting a suitable home.

1. Woodchester Roman Pavement

Rodborough Common

Pleasant open common land on high ground between the Avon Valley and the Golden Valley. Rodborough Fort, a turreted Victorian house, has a well run caravan site beside it . . . a good centre for touring the southern Cotswolds.

Stroud

Built on the steep slopes of the Frome (or Golden) Valley, Stroud has retained considerable character despite its industrialisation in the late 18th and early 19th centuries. It had in fact established itself as the pre-eminent centre of the Cotswold cloth industry as early as the 15th century, and the availability of Cotswold wool, of water for washing and of minerals for dyeing and cleaning, ensured that it remained so for several hundred years. High quality cloth is still produced here, but only in about six mills. However various industries have come here to replace cloth, and Stroud and its surrounding valley country is still bustling with activity. Visitors should concentrate on the Parish Church, a Victorian building with several earlier monuments, and a fine 14th century tower; and the interesting little Stroud Museum, which tells the story of Stroud's achievements as a cloth and industrial centre.

2. Stratford Park, Stroud

Haresfield Beacon

There is a topograph, or viewing table, in the Shortwood area (walk to left of our diversion road after .5) and .5 beyond this, car parking space for those who wish to walk along to Haresfield Beacon itself, a hill top surmounted by an Iron Age promontory fort. Splendid views from both points.

3. At Cud Hill

Edge

Small village with views westwards over the Severn valley, and eastwards to Painswick.

Painswick Beacon

Attractive open country with pine trees, old quarries, and a golf course nearby. If you value tranquility avoid Sunday afternoons.

4. Painswick Beacon

13

MAP 7

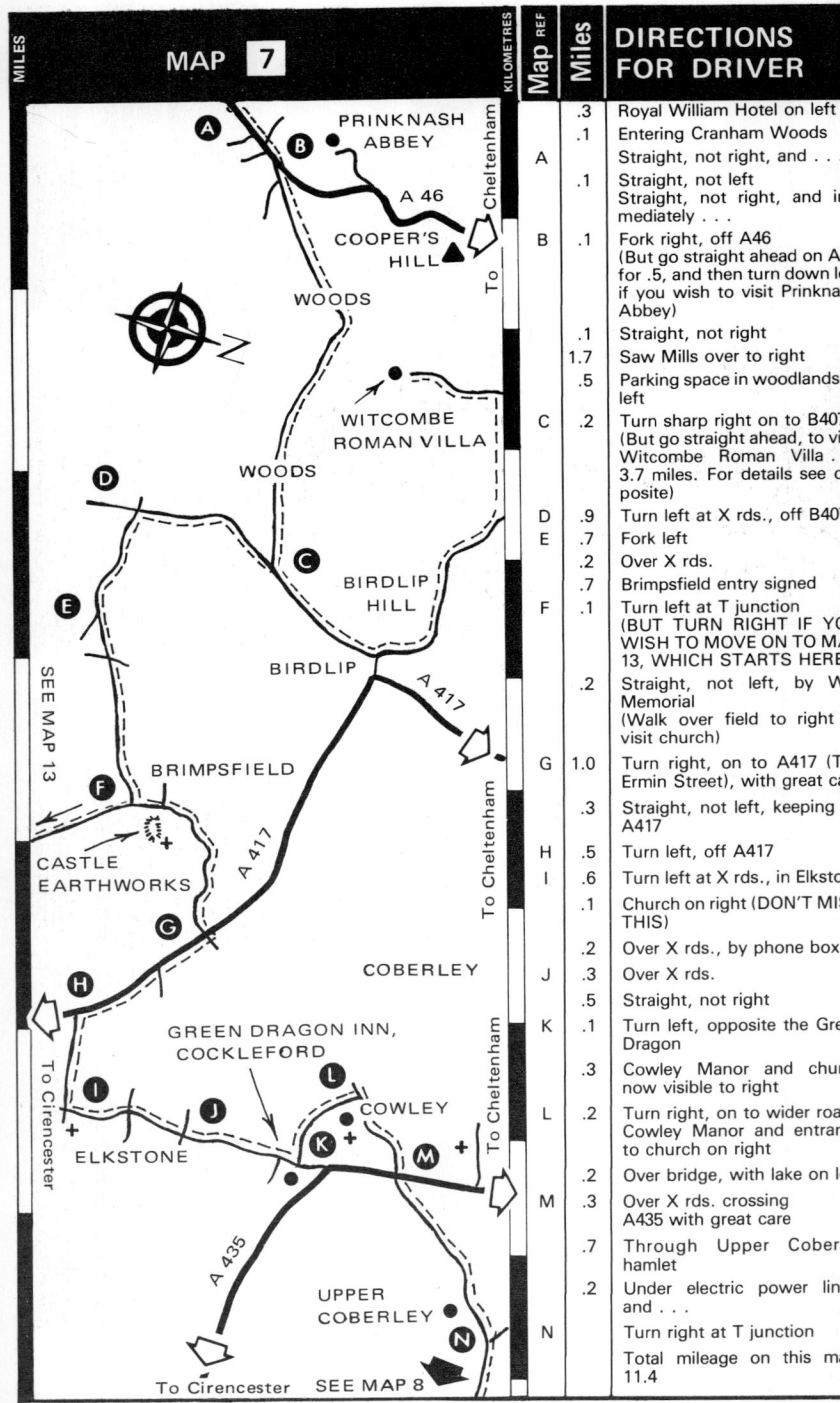

Map REF	Miles	DIRECTIONS FOR DRIVER	FOLLOW SIGN MARKED
	.3	Royal William Hotel on left	
	.1	Entering Cranham Woods	
A		Straight, not right, and . . .	Cheltenham
	.1	Straight, not left	Cheltenham
		Straight, not right, and immediately . . .	
B	.1	Fork right, off A46 (But go straight ahead on A46 for .5, and then turn down left if you wish to visit Prinknash Abbey)	Cranham
	.1	Straight, not right	Birdlip
	1.7	Saw Mills over to right	
	.5	Parking space in woodlands to left	
C	.2	Turn sharp right on to B4070 (But go straight ahead, to visit Witcombe Roman Villa . . . 3.7 miles. For details see opposite)	Sheepscombe
D	.9	Turn left at X rds., off B4070	Brimpsfield
E	.7	Fork left	Brimpsfield
	.2	Over X rds.	Brimpsfield
	.7	Brimpsfield entry signed	
F	.1	Turn left at T junction (BUT TURN RIGHT IF YOU WISH TO MOVE ON TO MAP 13, WHICH STARTS HERE)	Birdlip
	.2	Straight, not left, by War Memorial (Walk over field to right to visit church)	Cirencester
G	1.0	Turn right, on to A417 (The Ermin Street), with great care	Elkstone
	.3	Straight, not left, keeping on A417	No sign
H	.5	Turn left, off A417	Elkstone
I	.6	Turn left at X rds., in Elkstone	No sign
	.1	Church on right (DON'T MISS THIS)	
	.2	Over X rds., by phone box	Cowley
J	.3	Over X rds.	Cockleford
	.5	Straight, not right	No sign
K	.1	Turn left, opposite the Green Dragon	No sign
	.3	Cowley Manor and church now visible to right	
L	.2	Turn right, on to wider road Cowley Manor and entrance to church on right	No sign
	.2	Over bridge, with lake on left	
M	.3	Over X rds. crossing A435 with great care	Upper Coberley
	.7	Through Upper Coberley hamlet	
	.2	Under electric power lines, and . . .	
N		Turn right at T junction	No sign
		Total mileage on this map: 11.6	

CROWN COPYRIGHT RESERVED

14

PLACES OF INTEREST ON THE ROUTE

Prinknash Abbey

Its establishment dates from 1928, when a Benedictine community moved here from Caldey Island. However the 'old abbey', which shelters below wooded hillsides, with views out over the Severn plain, was built here in the 14th century, as a grange of the Abbots of Gloucester. The new monastic building is now complete, and visitors are encouraged to look round the well known pottery. There is also an attractive Bird Garden in part of the abbey grounds.

1. Prinknash.....The 'Old' Abbey

Buckholt, Cranham and Witcombe Woods

Beyond Point B our road goes through glorious woodlands, with beech predominating, for almost three miles. Parking opportunities are unfortunately very limited.

Diversion to Witcombe Roman Villa

(Go straight ahead at Point C . . . turn left after .8 . . . down Birdlip Hill with great care . . . after 1.7 bear left on to A417 by the Twelve Bells Inn . . . after .1 turn left off A417, following sign marked Droys Court . . . after .4 bear left at Droys Court . . . after .7 arrive at farm, where key to villa may be collected . . . only a few yards walk beyond.)

This is a 1st century Roman villa, with a small mosaic pavement and various items from the excavation displayed in a small building on the site.

Brimpsfield

There was a large castle here, but it was demolished in the 14th century, when its owner John Giffard crossed Edward II's path, and it was never re-built. However the earthworks are still visible in trees to the right of our path to the church. This is situated on the edge of the village, in a large churchyard with many 18th century tombstones. It has a 15th century tower which 'descends' into the centre of the building, providing us with a fascinating architectural puzzle.

2. In Witcombe Wood

Elkstone

Small village with a handsome 18th century rectory and an outstandingly interesting Norman church. There is a Norman south doorway, with tympanum and beak heads, and a beautiful little stone vaulted Norman chancel. See also the fine Perpendicular tower, the box pews, and the 17th century table tombs near the south porch. DON'T MISS THIS.

3. Brimpsfield Church

Cockleford

Hamlet blessed with an inn serving really good bread and cheese, and draught Guinness . . . the Green Dragon . . . an excellent place, happily remembered.

Cowley

Cowley Manor a 19th century Italianate mansion in exquisite gardens with lake and ornamental ponds, is now used by Gloucester County Council for various educational activities. The church, lying beside the manor, is not very interesting.

Upper Coberley

Attractive hamlet overlooking the upper Churn valley, with several open fronted barns . . . all supported on stone columns.

4. The Green Dragon, Cockleford

15

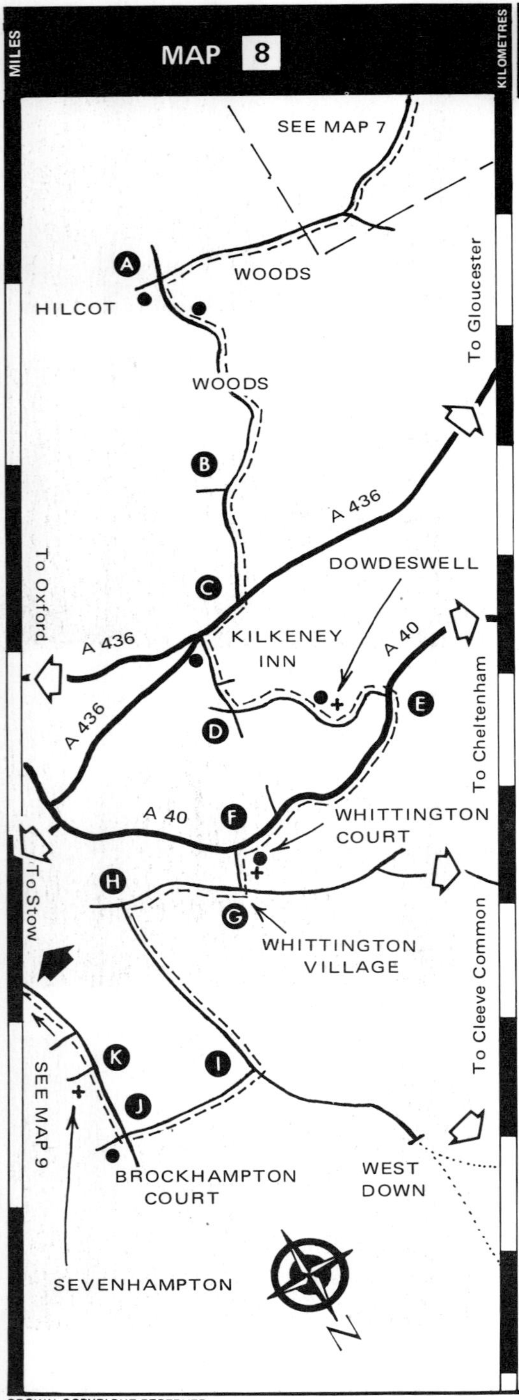

MAP 8

Map REF	Miles	DIRECTIONS FOR DRIVER	FOLLOW SIGN MARKED
	.1	Pleasant beech woods to left (Hilcot Wood)	
A	.9	Turn left at X rds.	Kilkenny
	.3	Upper Hilcot Farm on left	
	.2	Over bridge and into pleasant woodlands	
B	1.0	Straight, not right, just beyond woodland	No sign
C	.7	Bear right with care, on to A436 by old quarries on right	Andoversford
	.2	Turn sharp left, off A436, by the Kilkeney Inn	Dowdeswell
	.3	Straight, not left, at T junction	No sign
D	.2	Turn left at X rds.	Dowdeswell
	.6	Dowdeswell Court and Church on left	
	.1	Attractive house up right	
E	.2	Turn right, with care, on to A40	Oxford
	1.0	Straight, not right, keeping on A40	No sign
F	.3	Turn left, off A40, and Whittington Court and Church on left	Whittington
G	.2	Turn right in Whittington (But turn left if you wish to explore up to Cleeve Common . . . 3.6 miles. For details see opposite)	Brockhampton
	.1	Well head on right	
H	.5	Bear left at T junction	Whitehall
I	1.2	Turn right at T junction (But go straight ahead if you wish to explore up to West Down (Cleeve Common) . . . 1 mile)	Brockhampto
J	.8	Turn right at X rds. by Brockhampton Park (But go straight ahead if you wish to visit Brockhampton hamlet)	Sevenhampto
K	.5	Straight, not left, just beyond Sevenhampton Manor (But turn left if you wish to visit church)	Whittington
	.1	Straight, not left (But walk down left if you wish to visit Sevenhampton village)	Whittington
		Total mileage on this map: 9.5	

CROWN COPYRIGHT RESERVED

PLACES OF INTEREST ON THE ROUTE

Hilcot Wood and Pinchley Wood
A delightful, little known area of woodland in a valley which gives birth to the Hilcot brook, a tributary of the Churn. Upper Hilcot farmhouse is (unusually) half timbered.

Dowdeswell
Agreeably sited on a hillside, and happily just away from the busy A40. The church, with its small stone spire is situated below the road, beside a Tudor farmhouse. Inside there are two mid-19th century galleries, one for the manor and one for the rectory; a 16th century brass of a priest and a handsome monument on the chancel wall (William Rogers, 1734).

Whittington
Here are pleasant rows of cottages, a Victorian wayside well inscribed 'Waste not, want not', and well away from the village, a small church sheltering beneath the high walls of the romantic 16th century Whittington Court. The church, which has some Norman details, has a small bellcote and a pretty little north porch. However the most interesting treasures here are the three 14th century effigies, with two knights and one lady. Do not miss the brass to Richard Cotton and his wife, the builders of Whittington Court; nor the two little head stops to the arcading . . . a lady and gentlemen, who both look most Chaucerian.

Diversions to Cleeve Common
1. (Turn left at Point G . . . after .8 turn right beyond Whalley Farm and drive N.W. and W. for 2.8, to arrive at small car park just beyond gate by Radio Station.)
From this point one can walk northwards along the 'edge' to Cleeve Hill, or east to Wontley Farm and beyond to Belas Knap (see Book 2). Splendid open country this, with fine views over Cheltenham towards the Malverns.
2. (Go straight ahead at Point I for 1 mile to arrive at car park on edge of West Down.)
Walk N.W. from here to link with car park by Radio Station (see above, or north to Wontley Farm and on to Belas Knap (see book 2). (Use 1:50,000 O.S. Map No. 163 if possible).

Brockhampton
Hamlet with a large, 19th century mansion, Brockhampton Park, and an inn called the Craven Arms, very tucked away. The lovely River Colne, a tributary of the Thames, rises just to the north of Brockhampton.

Sevenhampton
Has a small ford in a valley overlooked by modest cottages, and nearer our road, a Norman church, altered and improved by the benefaction of John Camber, a rich wool merchant, who died in 1497. Flowering rock plants line the path to the south door, and inside John Camber's Perpendicular tower has provided another fascinating architectural story, with flying buttresses within the church, and vaulting high up above the crossing.

1. Farm at Hilcot

2. Dowdeswell Church

3. Whittington Court

4. Cottage at Sevenhampton

MAP 9

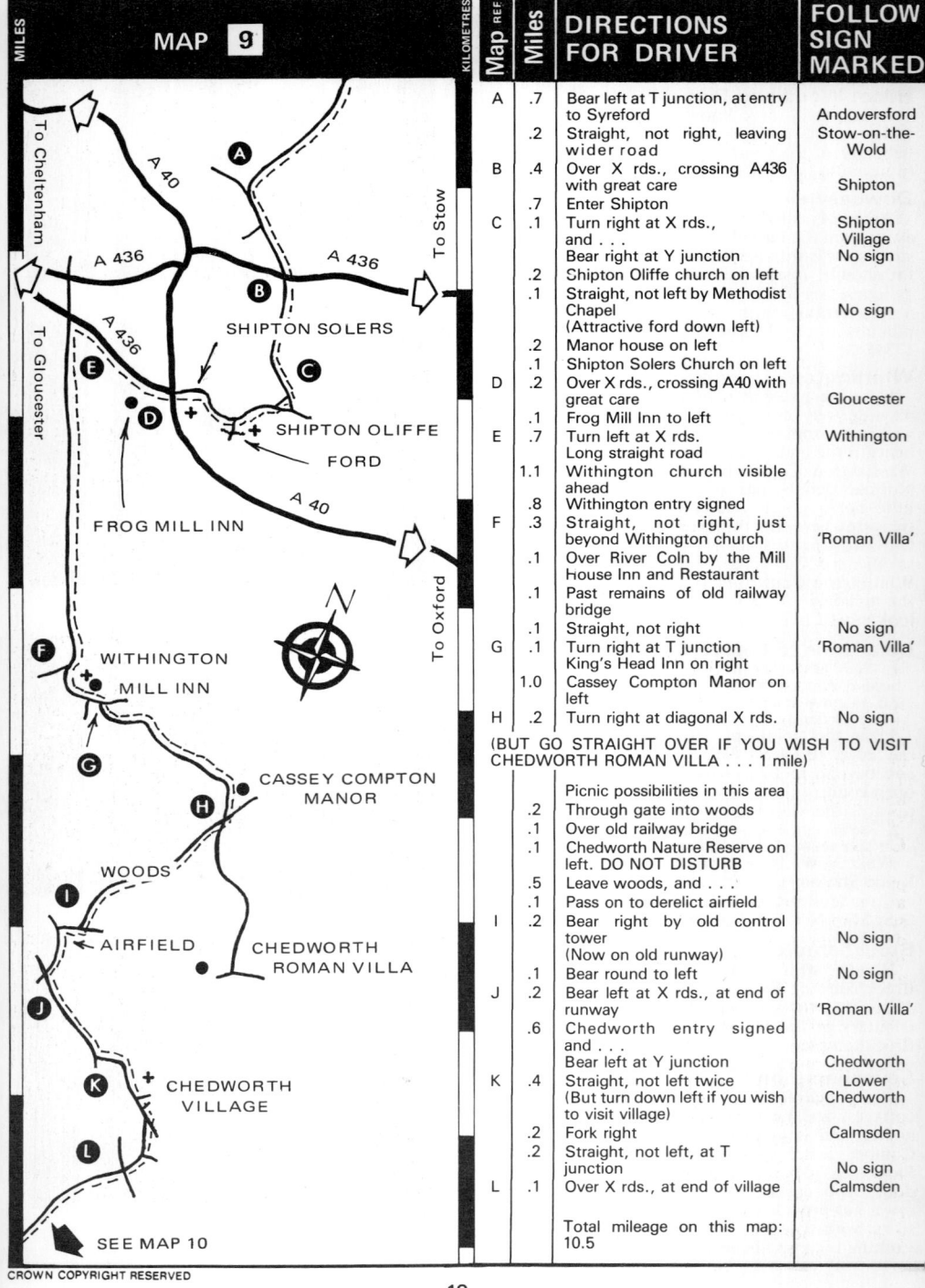

Map features labels: To Cheltenham, A 40, A 436, To Stow, To Gloucester, SHIPTON SOLERS, SHIPTON OLIFFE, FORD, FROG MILL INN, A 40, To Oxford, WITHINGTON MILL INN, CASSEY COMPTON MANOR, WOODS, AIRFIELD, CHEDWORTH ROMAN VILLA, CHEDWORTH VILLAGE, SEE MAP 10.

CROWN COPYRIGHT RESERVED

Map REF	Miles	DIRECTIONS FOR DRIVER	FOLLOW SIGN MARKED
A	.7	Bear left at T junction, at entry to Syreford	Andoversford
	.2	Straight, not right, leaving wider road	Stow-on-the-Wold
B	.4	Over X rds., crossing A436 with great care	Shipton
	.7	Enter Shipton	
C	.1	Turn right at X rds., and . . .	Shipton Village
		Bear right at Y junction	No sign
	.2	Shipton Oliffe church on left	
	.1	Straight, not left by Methodist Chapel (Attractive ford down left)	No sign
	.2	Manor house on left	
	.1	Shipton Solers Church on left	
D	.2	Over X rds., crossing A40 with great care	Gloucester
	.1	Frog Mill Inn to left	
E	.7	Turn left at X rds. Long straight road	Withington
	1.1	Withington church visible ahead	
	.8	Withington entry signed	
F	.3	Straight, not right, just beyond Withington church	'Roman Villa'
	.1	Over River Coln by the Mill House Inn and Restaurant	
	.1	Past remains of old railway bridge	
	.1	Straight, not right	No sign
G	.1	Turn right at T junction King's Head Inn on right	'Roman Villa'
	1.0	Cassey Compton Manor on left	
H	.2	Turn right at diagonal X rds.	No sign
(BUT GO STRAIGHT OVER IF YOU WISH TO VISIT CHEDWORTH ROMAN VILLA . . . 1 mile)
		Picnic possibilities in this area	
	.2	Through gate into woods	
	.1	Over old railway bridge	
	.1	Chedworth Nature Reserve on left. DO NOT DISTURB	
	.5	Leave woods, and . . .	
	.1	Pass on to derelict airfield	
I	.2	Bear right by old control tower (Now on old runway)	No sign
	.1	Bear round to left	No sign
J	.2	Bear left at X rds., at end of runway	'Roman Villa'
	.6	Chedworth entry signed and . . .	
		Bear left at Y junction	Chedworth
K	.4	Straight, not left twice (But turn down left if you wish to visit village)	Lower Chedworth
	.2	Fork right	Calmsden
	.2	Straight, not left, at T junction	No sign
L	.1	Over X rds., at end of village	Calmsden
		Total mileage on this map: 10.5	

PLACES OF INTEREST ON THE ROUTE

Shipton Oliffe
Long village on a small tributary of the Coln, with a minute ford, a startling Methodist chapel in bright red brick, and a pretty church overlooking ornamental gardens by the stream. It has all been rather tidied up inside, but we particularly liked the colourful Royal Arms in plaster relief.

Shipton Solers
Smaller than Oliffe, but the manor house's stream-side gardens are equally enchanting, and the little church just above our road was very sympathetically restored in 1929.

Withington
A pleasant, bustling village situated near the head of the beautiful Coln valley (see Book 2). There is a large church with partly Norman tower, blocked Norman north doorway, and fine Norman south doorway. The interior has been over restored, but don't miss the wall monument to Sir John and Lady Howe of Cassey Compton (see below), complete with their eight children. We have fond memories of vast log fires, shove-halfpenny, and excellent bread and cheese, at the hospitable Mill Inn.

Cassey Compton
Partly demolished 17th century mansion, now a large farmhouse. Note the pleasing roof lines of the house and buildings as you drop down the hill beyond Withington.

Chedworth Roman Villa
Owes its discovery in 1864 to an over ambitious ferret which had to be dug out of a rabbit warren, thus revealing various mosaic fragments. The villa is now owned by the National Trust, who maintain the interesting remains and an excellent small museum. The delightful woodland setting proves once again how adept the Romans were in the siting of their villas.

Chedworth Woods and Airfield
Our road beyond Cassey Compton cross roads passes through the extensive Chedworth woods . . . a beautiful area with a pleasing blend of hard and soft woods. Beyond the woods we pass through the deserted hutments of Chedworth airfield, beside the old control tower, and along one of the runways . . . a sad nostalgic place.

Chedworth
Large village, once neatly dissected by a branch line, complete with tall viaduct, and whose closure only the most fanatical railway enthusiast could deplore. The attractive part of the village centres upon the Seven Tuns Inn, the spring bubbling out of a wall opposite, and the interesting late Norman church a short distance beyond. This was considerably enriched during the Perpendicular period, and light floods in through tall windows on the south side, on to the stout Norman tub font, and (in contrast) on to the elegant 15th century stone pulpit. Do not miss the lovely modern sculpture of a Virgin and Child (1911).

1. Ford at Shipton Oliffe

2. Cassey Compton Manor

3. At Chedworth Roman Villa

4. Font at Chedworth

MAP 10

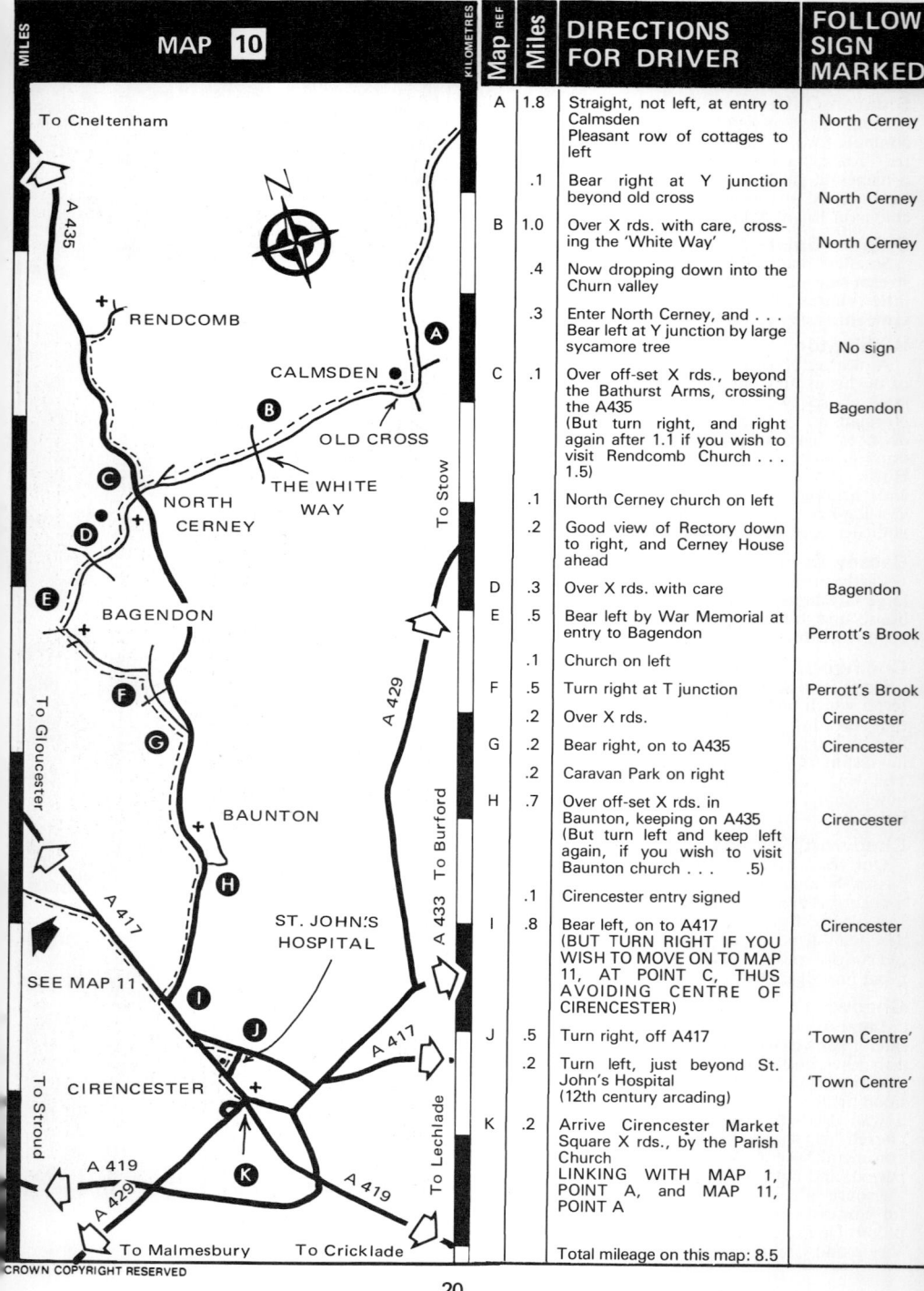

Map REF	Miles	DIRECTIONS FOR DRIVER	FOLLOW SIGN MARKED
A	1.8	Straight, not left, at entry to Calmsden Pleasant row of cottages to left	North Cerney
	.1	Bear right at Y junction beyond old cross	North Cerney
B	1.0	Over X rds. with care, crossing the 'White Way'	North Cerney
	.4	Now dropping down into the Churn valley	
	.3	Enter North Cerney, and . . . Bear left at Y junction by large sycamore tree	No sign
C	.1	Over off-set X rds., beyond the Bathurst Arms, crossing the A435 (But turn right, and right again after 1.1 if you wish to visit Rendcomb Church . . . 1.5)	Bagendon
	.1	North Cerney church on left	
	.2	Good view of Rectory down to right, and Cerney House ahead	
D	.3	Over X rds. with care	Bagendon
E	.5	Bear left by War Memorial at entry to Bagendon	Perrott's Brook
	.1	Church on left	
F	.5	Turn right at T junction	Perrott's Brook
	.2	Over X rds.	Cirencester
G	.2	Bear right, on to A435	Cirencester
	.2	Caravan Park on right	
H	.7	Over off-set X rds. in Baunton, keeping on A435 (But turn left and keep left again, if you wish to visit Baunton church . . . .5)	Cirencester
	.1	Cirencester entry signed	
I	.8	Bear left, on to A417 (BUT TURN RIGHT IF YOU WISH TO MOVE ON TO MAP 11, AT POINT C, THUS AVOIDING CENTRE OF CIRENCESTER)	Cirencester
J	.5	Turn right, off A417	'Town Centre'
	.2	Turn left, just beyond St. John's Hospital (12th century arcading)	'Town Centre'
K	.2	Arrive Cirencester Market Square X rds., by the Parish Church LINKING WITH MAP 1, POINT A, and MAP 11, POINT A	
		Total mileage on this map: 8.5	

CROWN COPYRIGHT RESERVED

PLACES OF INTEREST ON THE ROUTE

Calmsden
Agreeable little hamlet with a row of attractively glazed early 19th century cottages, and a 14th century wayside cross, with a spring below the grassy bank on which it stands.

The White Way
A minor Roman road serving the various villas that lay between Cirencester and the Cotswold edge in the vicinity of Winchcombe.

North Cerney
Pleasant village in the Churn valley, with the Bathurst Arms set in a stream-side garden, and looking across the busy A435 to the little saddle-back tower of the largely Norman church. This is an exquisitely restored and re-furnished building, thanks to the generosity of Mr. W. I. Croome. Much of this was carried out by F. C. Eden, whose work we first encountered at Blisland on the remote western fringes of Bodmin Moor. See especially the Norman south doorway, the roof with its fascinating corbel figures, the handsome gallery, the beautiful medieval glass, and the lovely monument to Thomas Tyndale in the Lady Chapel. See also the late 17th century Rectory opposite and Cerney House beyond.

Rendcomb Church
(Turn right at Point C . . . follow up A435 for 1.1 . . . then turn right, and drive up to church.)

A largely Perpendicular building thanks to the munificence of Sir Edmund Tame, wool merchant of Fairford, and son of John Tame, who built the magnificent church there. See especially the stained glass, the 16th century screen (an unusual feature in the Cotswolds), and above all, the splendid Norman font with figures of the apostles beneath arcades, with Judas left uncarved.

Bagendon
Small village in a sheltered valley. The over-restored church is all on a very small scale, with Norman saddle-back tower and Norman arcading. The chancel is much higher than the nave, and was made so in medieval times to avoid flooding. See especially the handsome little 'Rector's Roll', and the window in the north wall of the chancel. Bagendon Dykes, to the south and west of the village, are the remains of the Belgic (Iron Age) capital of the Dobunni, which flourished here immediately before the coming of the Romans, who 'civilized' the tribes by moving them into Roman style provincial capitals . . . in this case Cirencester (Corinium Dobunnorum).

Baunton
Straggling village to the immediate north of Cirencester, and too close to preserve much of its individuality. However the small church lies quietly away from the main road. It has a heavily restored interior, but should not be missed, as it contains a remarkable 14th century wall painting of St. Christopher. See also the richly embroidered 15th century altar frontal.

1. Cottages at Calmsden

2. Calmsden Cross

3. Springtime at North Cerney

4. St. John's Hospital Cirencester

5. Entrance to Cirencester Park

21

MAP 11

Map REF	Miles	DIRECTIONS FOR DRIVER	FOLLOW SIGN MARKED
A		Leave X rds., by Cirencester Parish Church, northwards, up 'West Market Place', and . . .	Gloucester
		Bear right, beyond Church	Gloucester
	.2	Turn right, down Spitalgate Lane, and pass St. John's Hospital on left	Gloucester
B	.1	Turn left, on to A417	Gloucester
C	.6	Straight, not right, at Y junction, keeping on A417	Gloucester
		(THIS POINT IS COMMON WITH MAP 10, POINT I)	
	.2	Plough Inn, on left (Now in Stratton)	
D	.4	Fork left, off A417, by War Memorial	Daglingworth
	.1	Stratton Church on left	
	.9	Daglingworth entry signed	
	.1	Straight, not left	No sign
	.2	Dovecot in garden over to left	
	.1	Over X rds. (But turn left if you wish to visit church)	Sapperton
E	.1	Straight, not right	Sapperton
		(WE ARE JOINED HERE FROM THE END OF MAP 13)	
	.2	Straight, not right, at Y junction	Sapperton
	.7	Enter Cirencester Park Woodland area	
	.2	Entry on left to Cirencester Park, for walkers and riders. Please read notice before using path	
	.4	Overley Ride crosses the road	
F	.6	Turn left at T junction, at 'Park Corner'	Sapperton
G	1.2	Turn right at T junction (But go just beyond for open space to left, where Broad Ride crosses road. Fine gates well up to left)	Sapperton
	.1	Sapperton entry signed	
	.2	Bear left by church	No sign
	.2	Straight, not right by school	No sign
H	.1	Bear right at diagonal X rds., and down steep hill	Daneway
		Over old canal bridge, and . . .	
I	.4	Bear left by the Daneway Inn (But bear right to look at Daneway House... .2. Only open to parties by appointment)	Waterlane
	.2	Fine views back down valley to Daneway	
	.1	Attractive little lodge to right Pleasant woodland country beyond	
		Total mileage on this map: 7.6	

CROWN COPYRIGHT RESERVED

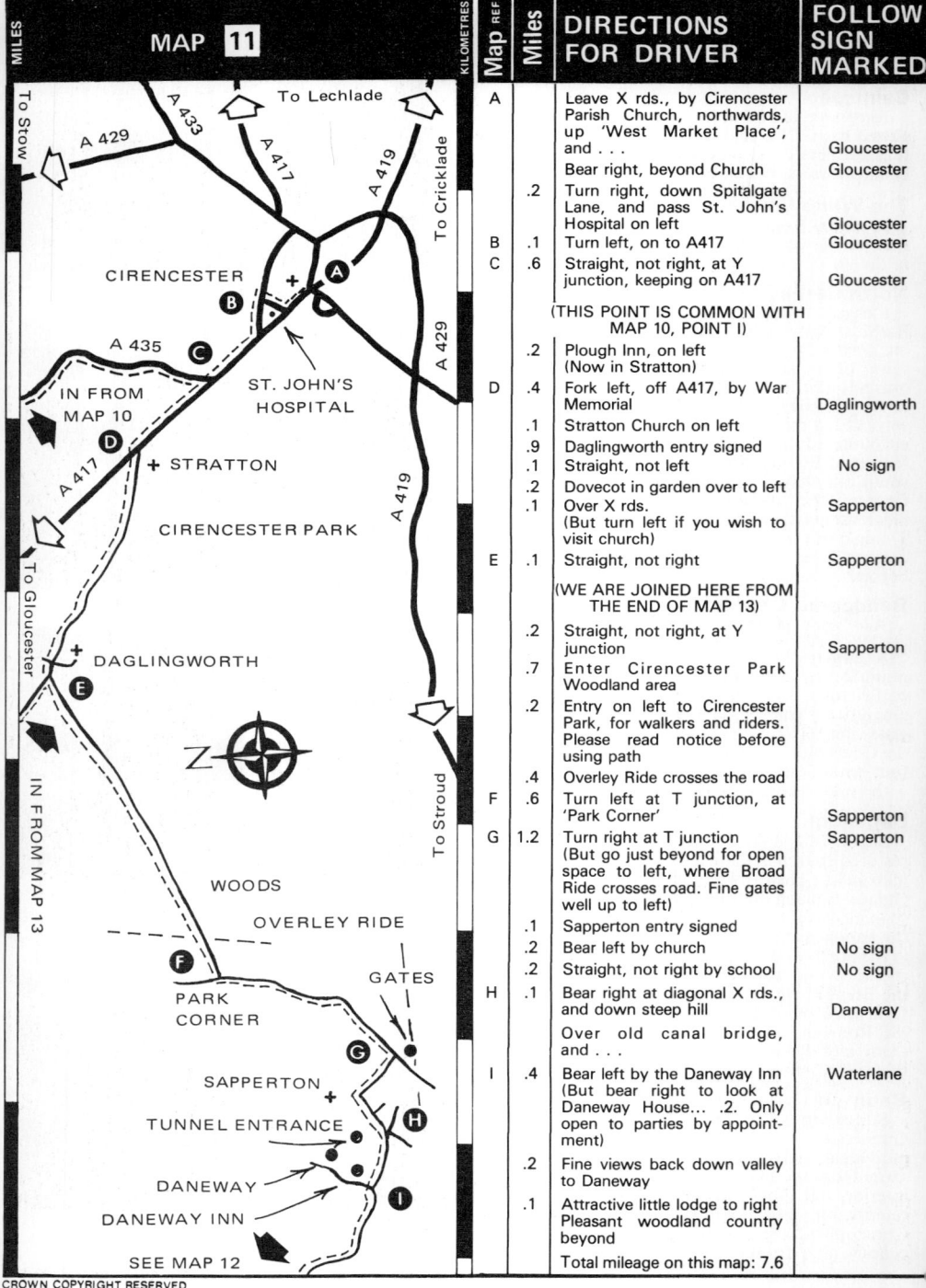

22

PLACES OF INTEREST ON THE ROUTE

Stratton
Lies on the Ermin Street (hence the name Stratton), and is almost a suburb of Cirencester. The small church has a Perpendicular door and doorway let into a large Norman opening, which still has a carved tympanum above it.

Daglingworth
The charmingly sited church and rectory stand well above the rest of the village. The church has a Saxon doorway, and part of a Roman altar, re-used by the Saxons, who made it into a window. The three carvings set into the walls were rediscovered in 1850 and form a unique group of primitive Saxon sculpture. See also the interesting Saxon sundial over the doorway, and the fine 15th century door itself.

In the grounds of the manor there is an interesting dovecot, which has a revolving ladder to give access to all 500 nesting places.

1. & 2. Sculptures at Daglingworth

Cirencester Park
The mansion, which lies at the town end of the park, was built by the First Earl Bathurst in 1714 – 18, and is not open to the public. However, as for the park, notices proclaim. 'YOU ARE WELCOME ON FOOT AND ON HORSEBACK BY PERMISSION OF THE EARL BATHURST. DOGS, CARS, CYCLES OR UNACCOMPANIED CHILDREN ARE NOT ALLOWED. TAKE YOUR LITTER HOME'. The Broad Ride is nearly five miles long and stretches westwards from the town, almost to Sapperton. Wander at will in great woodlands and open parkland, but always remember that you are a privileged guest, and not there by right.

3. Cirencester Park Gate, near Sapperton

Sapperton
Trim little village poised above the deep Frome valley, with an attractive terrace road beyond the church. This lies at the bottom of a long sloping path beneath yew trees, and is a largely 18th century building, having round headed windows with their original glass, and a very stylish interior including much Jacobean woodwork. There are two very fine monuments here . . . Sir Henry Poole and family (1616), and Sir Robert Atkyns (1711).

4. & 5. Monuments at Sapperton

Daneway
Here below Sapperton, was the north western end of the Thames and Severn Canal's long tunnel from Coates (see page 3). The Daneway Inn, like the Tunnel House Inn at the Coates end, must have provided countless thousands of pints for the thirsty leggers during the tunnel's short working life between 1789 and 1911.

Daneway House
A fascinating Cotswold manor house dating from the 14th century, which was used by the Barnsley brothers and Ernest Gimson (all disciples of William Morris) as furniture workshops and showrooms for about twenty years.

6. The Daneway Inn, near Sapperton

MAP 12

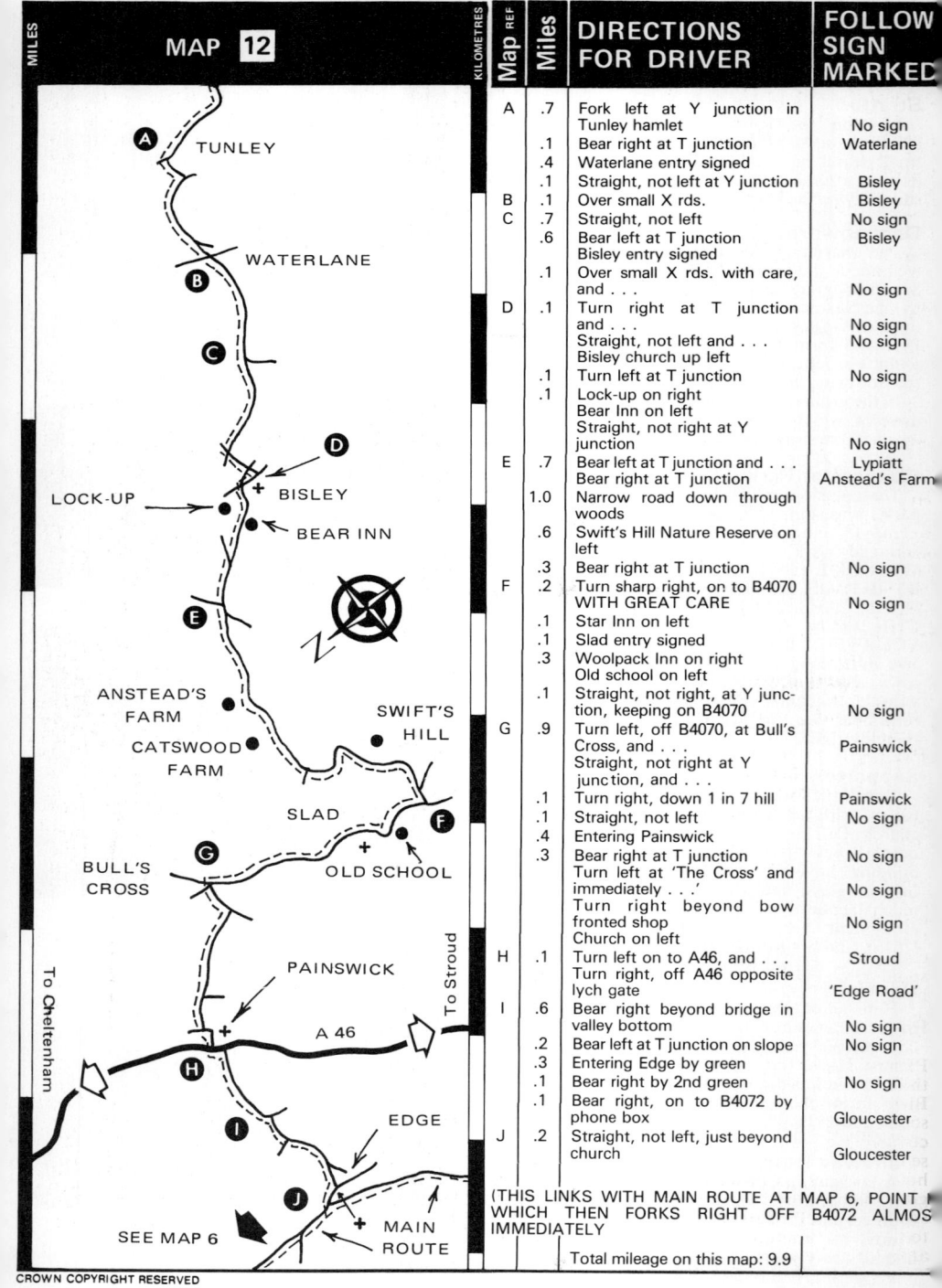

Map REF	Miles	DIRECTIONS FOR DRIVER	FOLLOW SIGN MARKED
A	.7	Fork left at Y junction in Tunley hamlet	No sign
	.1	Bear right at T junction	Waterlane
	.4	Waterlane entry signed	
	.1	Straight, not left at Y junction	Bisley
B	.1	Over small X rds.	Bisley
C	.7	Straight, not left	No sign
	.6	Bear left at T junction Bisley entry signed	Bisley
	.1	Over small X rds. with care, and . . .	No sign
D	.1	Turn right at T junction and . . .	No sign
		Straight, not left and . . . Bisley church up left	No sign
	.1	Turn left at T junction	No sign
	.1	Lock-up on right Bear Inn on left Straight, not right at Y junction	No sign
E	.7	Bear left at T junction and . . .	Lypiatt
		Bear right at T junction	Anstead's Farm
	1.0	Narrow road down through woods	
	.6	Swift's Hill Nature Reserve on left	
	.3	Bear right at T junction	No sign
F	.2	Turn sharp right, on to B4070 WITH GREAT CARE	No sign
	.1	Star Inn on left	
	.1	Slad entry signed	
	.3	Woolpack Inn on right Old school on left	
	.1	Straight, not right, at Y junction, keeping on B4070	No sign
G	.9	Turn left, off B4070, at Bull's Cross, and . . .	Painswick
		Straight, not right at Y junction, and . . .	
	.1	Turn right, down 1 in 7 hill	Painswick
	.1	Straight, not left	No sign
	.4	Entering Painswick	
	.3	Bear right at T junction	No sign
		Turn left at 'The Cross' and immediately . . .	No sign
		Turn right beyond bow fronted shop	No sign
		Church on left	
H	.1	Turn left on to A46, and . . .	Stroud
		Turn right, off A46 opposite lych gate	'Edge Road'
I	.6	Bear right beyond bridge in valley bottom	No sign
	.2	Bear left at T junction on slope	No sign
	.3	Entering Edge by green	
	.1	Bear right by 2nd green	No sign
	.1	Bear right, on to B4072 by phone box	Gloucester
J	.2	Straight, not left, just beyond church	Gloucester

(THIS LINKS WITH MAIN ROUTE AT MAP 6, POINT I WHICH THEN FORKS RIGHT OFF B4072 ALMOST IMMEDIATELY

Total mileage on this map: 9.9

PLACES OF INTEREST ON THE ROUTE

Tunley
Small hamlet in a deeply wooded combe thrusting northwards from the Frome valley.

Waterlane
A scattered hamlet in high country beyond Tunley. There are several pleasant houses, but these do not lie on our road. All rather scrappy.

Bisley
This large village in upland country well to the north of the Golden Valley is a sheer delight. Everywhere one's eyes roam they are rewarded with good things. The clothiers of the valleys brought their wealth with them to Bisley, and spent wisely . . . on splendid houses like Over Court, with its charming 18th century gazebo, handsome Jaynes Court to the south west of the church, and the multitude of more modest, but equally pleasant houses and cottages. The church has a fine spire and a unique 13th century 'Poor Soul's Light' (England's only outdoor example), but the interior was over zealously restored by the Victorians. However do not overlook the effigy of a 13th century knight, nor the font with its Norman bowl and 19th century stem. Close to the delightful Bear Inn, with its stone support pillars, is a pretty little village lock-up (1824), and below the church is Bisley Wells, a Victorian restoration of seven springs, complete with Gothic detail.

Swift's Hill
This is now a Nature Reserve in the care of the Gloucestershire Trust for Nature Conservation, and is a pleasantly scrubby, grass covered area which should be left undisturbed as much as possible. However it is a quiet drive down through woodlands to this point, and there are mouth-watering views across the valley to Slad.

Slad
This small village strung out along the B4010, climbing up and along the valley out of Stroud, is inevitably linked with the poet and author Laurie Lee. It was here that he stored up the memories of childhood that were to be so brilliantly recalled in 'Cider with Rosie'. We pass the school and the church, but we have never stopped, never daring to spoil the memories of childhood bestowed upon us by Mr. Lee.

Painswick
Situated on a high spur between two valleys, Painswick is an elegant town, made prosperous by the clothing industry in the 17th and 18th centuries. Bisley is much quieter, but here we have a more sophisticated scene . . . the church with its fine 17th century spire, its famous clipped yews, and splendid series of table tombs . . . all this surrounded by houses, shops, hotels and inns, almost all in light grey stone, and many of which are embellished with small architectural details, bringing further pleasure to the eye. All we have to do is dispose of the A46 and we would have perfection.

1. Early Summer at Bisley

2. Bisley Lock-up

3. Gazebo at Bisley

4. Laurie Lee Country, Slad

5. The Cross, Painswick

6. Painswick Church

MAP 13

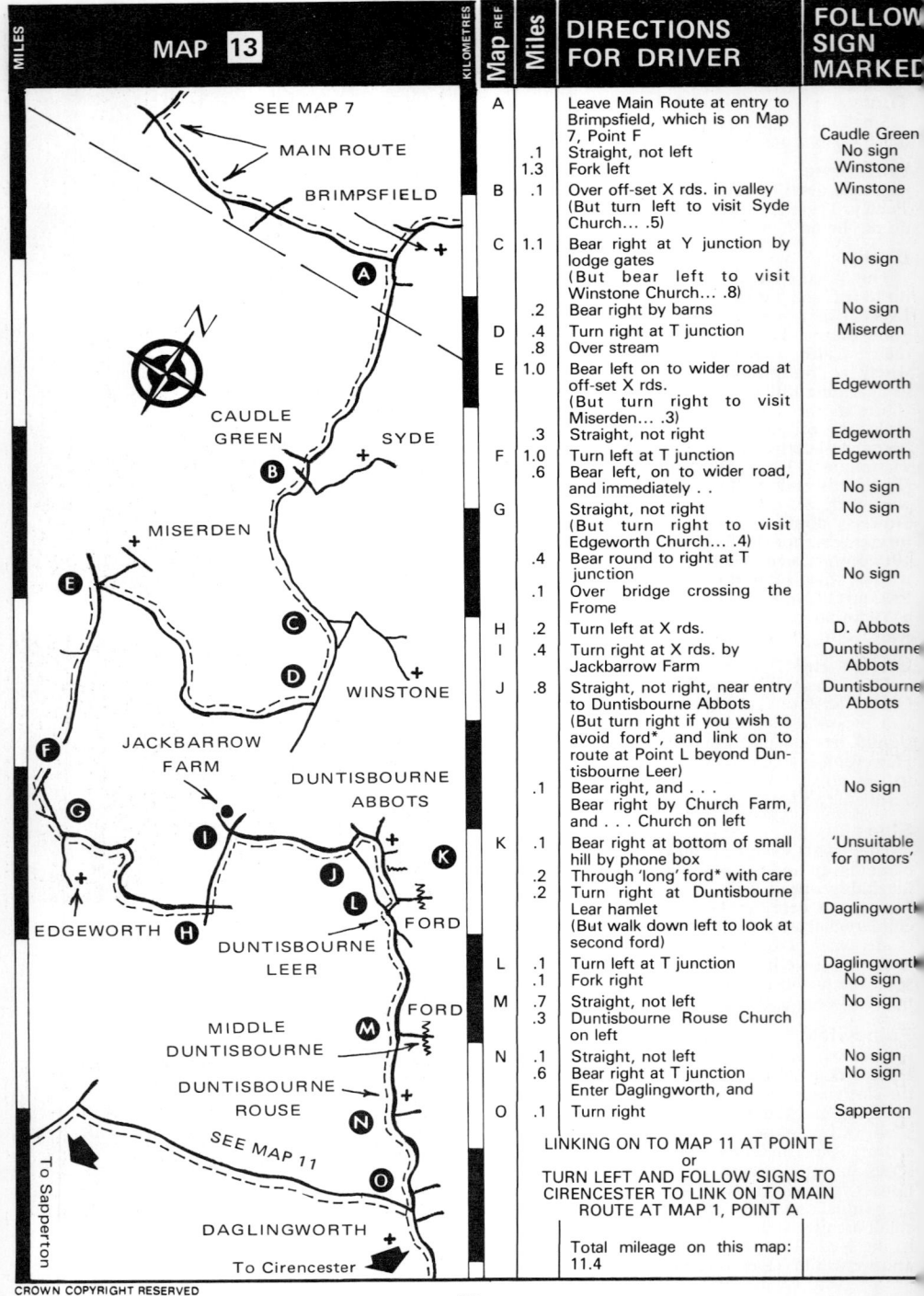

Map shows route through Brimsfield, Caudle Green, Syde, Miserden, Winston, Jackbarrow Farm, Edgeworth, Duntisbourne Abbots, Duntisbourne Leer, Middle Duntisbourne, Duntisbourne Rouse, Daglingworth, linking to Sapperton and Cirencester.

Map REF	Miles	DIRECTIONS FOR DRIVER	FOLLOW SIGN MARKED
A		Leave Main Route at entry to Brimpsfield, which is on Map 7, Point F	Caudle Green
	.1	Straight, not left	No sign
	1.3	Fork left	Winstone
B	.1	Over off-set X rds. in valley (But turn left to visit Syde Church... .5)	Winstone
C	1.1	Bear right at Y junction by lodge gates (But bear left to visit Winstone Church... .8)	No sign
	.2	Bear right by barns	No sign
D	.4	Turn right at T junction	Miserden
	.8	Over stream	
E	1.0	Bear left on to wider road at off-set X rds. (But turn right to visit Miserden... .3)	Edgeworth
	.3	Straight, not right	Edgeworth
F	1.0	Turn left at T junction	Edgeworth
	.6	Bear left, on to wider road, and immediately ..	No sign
G		Straight, not right (But turn right to visit Edgeworth Church... .4)	No sign
	.4	Bear round to right at T junction	No sign
	.1	Over bridge crossing the Frome	
H	.2	Turn left at X rds.	D. Abbots
I	.4	Turn right at X rds. by Jackbarrow Farm	Duntisbourne Abbots
J	.8	Straight, not right, near entry to Duntisbourne Abbots (But turn right if you wish to avoid ford*, and link on to route at Point L beyond Duntisbourne Leer)	Duntisbourne Abbots
	.1	Bear right, and . . . Bear right by Church Farm, and . . . Church on left	No sign
K	.1	Bear right at bottom of small hill by phone box	'Unsuitable for motors'
	.2	Through 'long' ford* with care	
	.2	Turn right at Duntisbourne Lear hamlet (But walk down left to look at second ford)	Daglingworth
L	.1	Turn left at T junction	Daglingworth
	.1	Fork right	No sign
M	.7	Straight, not left	No sign
	.3	Duntisbourne Rouse Church on left	
N	.1	Straight, not left	No sign
	.6	Bear right at T junction Enter Daglingworth, and	No sign
O	.1	Turn right	Sapperton

LINKING ON TO MAP 11 AT POINT E
or
TURN LEFT AND FOLLOW SIGNS TO CIRENCESTER TO LINK ON TO MAIN ROUTE AT MAP 1, POINT A

Total mileage on this map: 11.4

CROWN COPYRIGHT RESERVED

PLACES OF INTEREST ON THE ROUTE

Caudle Green
A hillside hamlet looking across a deep wooded valley to Syde, with a rough green overlooked by a pleasant 18th century farmhouse.

Syde
Quiet hamlet, looking across to Syde, with an early Norman church. This has a small saddle-backed tower and a pleasing 15th century roof, looking more like a barn's than a church's. The chancel is Victorian, but even this is pleasant. Do not overlook the 17th century box pews, nor the little 15th century glass roundel in muted colours, of St. James of Compostella. There is a tithe barn on the south side of the churchyard.

Winstone
A rather indeterminate upland village, with an unusually large number of farms within its bounds, but nothing of special interest apart from the church. This has an Anglo-Saxon blocked north doorway, and a chancel arch of the same period . . . both with typically massive jambs. Ruthlessly scraped interior . . . remains of 14th century cross outside south porch.

Miserden
A very trim largely 19th and 20th century estate village, with small octagonal shelter built around a massive sycamore tree, and overlooked by the hospitable Carpenter's Arms. The church has late Saxon origins and stands in a beautiful churchyard enriched with yew and beech. See especially the elaborately carved and gilded reredos and the splendid 17th century monuments.

Edgeworth
Has a church and manor house beautifully sited above the steep wooded slopes of the Frome valley. The interior of the church has been disastrously over restored, but don't miss the 14th century glass (of a bishop) in the chancel.

Duntisbourne Abbots
Another very trim village, with widespread evidence of much time and money being lavished upon its houses and cottages. The church's chancel has been very recently restored . . . white painted and rather pleasant . . . but the rest is still 'scraped' and somewhat severe. We like the ford beyond Point K, but you can avoid this if you wish (see Route Directions).

Duntisbourne Leer
The unusual name is derived from the Abbey of Lire in Normandy, to whom this parish originally belonged. Now only a hamlet, Duntisbourne Leer will be remembered chiefly for the farmhouse and buildings attractively grouped around the ford.

Duntisbourne Rouse (see page 29)

1. Syde Church *2. Cross at Winstone*

3. Monument at Miserden

4. Ford at Duntisbourne Leer

5. Duntisbourne Rouse Church

27

MAP 14

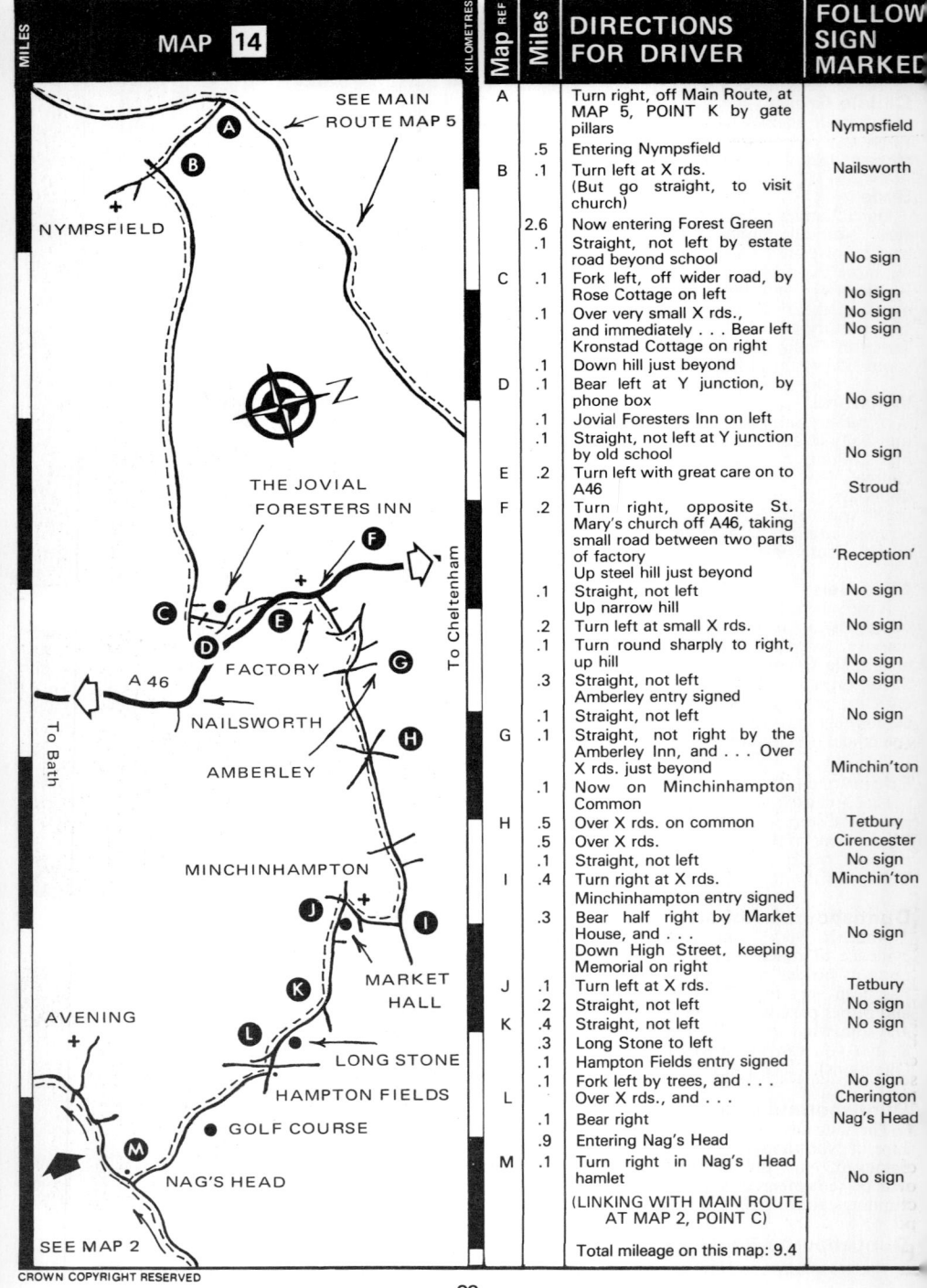

Map REF	Miles	DIRECTIONS FOR DRIVER	FOLLOW SIGN MARKED
A		Turn right, off Main Route, at MAP 5, POINT K by gate pillars	Nympsfield
	.5	Entering Nympsfield	
B	.1	Turn left at X rds. (But go straight, to visit church)	Nailsworth
	2.6	Now entering Forest Green	
	.1	Straight, not left by estate road beyond school	No sign
C	.1	Fork left, off wider road, by Rose Cottage on left	No sign
	.1	Over very small X rds., and immediately . . . Bear left Kronstad Cottage on right	No sign No sign
	.1	Down hill just beyond	
D	.1	Bear left at Y junction, by phone box	No sign
	.1	Jovial Foresters Inn on left	
	.1	Straight, not left at Y junction by old school	No sign
E	.2	Turn left with great care on to A46	Stroud
F	.2	Turn right, opposite St. Mary's church off A46, taking small road between two parts of factory	'Reception'
		Up steel hill just beyond	
	.1	Straight, not left Up narrow hill	No sign
	.2	Turn left at small X rds.	No sign
	.1	Turn round sharply to right, up hill	No sign
	.3	Straight, not left Amberley entry signed	No sign
	.1	Straight, not left	No sign
G	.1	Straight, not right by the Amberley Inn, and . . . Over X rds. just beyond	Minchin'ton
	.1	Now on Minchinhampton Common	
H	.5	Over X rds. on common	Tetbury
	.5	Over X rds.	Cirencester
	.1	Straight, not left	No sign
I	.4	Turn right at X rds. Minchinhampton entry signed	Minchin'ton
	.3	Bear half right by Market House, and . . . Down High Street, keeping Memorial on right	No sign
J	.1	Turn left at X rds.	Tetbury
	.2	Straight, not left	No sign
K	.4	Straight, not left	No sign
	.3	Long Stone to left	
	.1	Hampton Fields entry signed	
	.1	Fork left by trees, and . . .	No sign
L		Over X rds., and . . .	Cherington
	.1	Bear right	Nag's Head
	.9	Entering Nag's Head	
M	.1	Turn right in Nag's Head hamlet	No sign
		(LINKING WITH MAIN ROUTE AT MAP 2, POINT C)	
		Total mileage on this map: 9.4	

CROWN COPYRIGHT RESERVED

PLACES OF INTEREST ON THE ROUTE

Duntisbourne Rouse (see page 26)
A mainly Norman church standing in a sloping churchyard, with a fine 14th century cross for company. It has a pleasing interior, with box pews, stalls in the chancel with misericords, and medieval wall paintings. It is interesting to find that this is built upon such a slope, that there is a crypt at its eastern end . . . a most unusual feature in so small a church.

Nympsfield
Moderately attractive village sheltering just behind the high Cotswold edge, with a pleasant inn, the Rose and Crown, and a 19th century church. This has a Perpendicular tower complete with gargoyles, turret stair and a handsome clock face.

Forest Green, Windsoredge and Inchbrook
These are almost part of Nailsworth, but we gradually drop down through them to the valley, over a complicated series of small roads between houses and cottages on hillside terraces. Once in the valley we make use of the busy A46 for a mere .2, before turning off, through a factory, and up a steep hill towards Amberley. This is a real piece of 'White Horse' routing and if you wish to cross the valley in a more normal way, drive straight down into Nailsworth from Forest Hill, and follow signs to Michinhampton. We hope that you will stay with us.

Amberley
A scattered village on the high edge of Minchinhampton Common, with splendid views westwards out over the valley we have just crossed. Much of the novel John Halifax Gentleman was centred here . . . Mrs. Craik, its authoress lived at Rose Cottage.

Minchinhampton
Situated high up on the eastern edge of Minchinhampton Common (580 acres, now in the care of the National Trust), this is one of our favourite Cotswold cloth towns. Its beautiful High Street is almost as rich in the variety of its architectural styles as Chipping Campden. See especially the 18th century Crown Hotel, and the fascinating Market House, supported on its rows of stone and wood columns. The church overlooks the northern end of High Street, although it stands slightly aloof from it. It has a fine 14th century south transept and an unusually truncated spire (taken down to this height as long ago as 1563). Do not miss the vaulting beneath the tower, the interesting brasses, which include a pair of corpses in their shrouds, nor the screen and chancel roof . . . both by F. C. Eden (see North Cerney page 21).

The Long Stone
On the left of our road about a mile beyond Minchinhampton, this large standing stone may be one of the surviving stones of a long barrow burial chamber. There appears to have been a corresponding mound here in the late 18th century.

Hampton Fields (see page 31)

1. The Rose & Crown, Nympsfield

2. Our Road to Amberley

3. Minchinhampton

4. The Long Stone, beyond Michinhampton

MAP 15

Map Ref	Miles	DIRECTIONS FOR DRIVER	FOLLOW SIGN MARKED
A		Turn right, on to A4135 if you are leaving the Main Route at Map 2, Point J.	Dursley
		(This is in fact a small X rds., .8 from Tetbury out on the Dursley Road A4135)	
	.9	Beverstone entry signed	
	.2	Over small X rds. in village	No sign
B	.1	Straight, not right, by Beverstone Castle on right (But turn right, up very small lane, if you wish to visit Beverstone church)	No sign
C	1.7	Turn left at Calcot X rds. onto A46	Bath
	.5	Pleasant open road, with fine views over to left, as far as the Marlborough Downs	
D	.4	Turn right at small X rds. off A46	Kingscote
E	.7	Turn left at T junction by green barn	No sign
	.1	Round barrow visible well over to left	
	.1	Dropping down into valley. Newington Bagpath church, and castle earthworks visible across valley	
	.3	Through farmstead in valley	
	.1	Castle earthworks above us to left	
	.1	Newington Bagpath church on left	
F	.5	Turn right at T junction	No sign
G	.6	Turn left, onto A4135, and almost immediately	No sign
		Turn right, off A4135, by the Hunter's Hall Inn	Kingscote Village
	.2	Enter Kingscote	
H	.1	Turn left at T junction (But turn right if you wish to visit church)	'The Windmill'
	.7	Turn right, on to wider road	No sign
I	.1	Turn left, on to B4058	Wotton-under-Edge
J	.4	Turn right at X rds.	Uley
K	.1	Fork right, onto small road, towards asbestos barn (Watch for this with care)	No sign
	.1	Fine views over to left Narrow road	
	.4	Now starting steep descent through woods	
	.5	Owlpen Manor and church on right	
	.4	Enter Uley	
L	.2	Turn right, on to B4066	'Uley Tumulus'
		(JOINING THE MAIN ROUTE AT MAP 5, POINT I)	
		Total mileage on this map: 9.5	

CROWN COPYRIGHT RESERVED

PLACES OF INTEREST ON THE ROUTE

Hampton Fields (see page 28)
Hamlet with a pleasant row of late 18th and early 19th century stone cottages. Fine views of rolling country southwards, from our road beyond here.

Beverstone
Small village on the A4135, with several cottages built by Vulliamy for the Holfords who purchased the Beverstone estate in 1842 (see Westonbirt page 7). Here is one of the few surviving Cotswold castles . . . a 13th century building with 17th century domestic additions and alterations. It is not open to the public, but glimpses may be obtained from the main road, and from the little roadway up to the church. The latter has an interesting Anglo-Saxon sculpture of the Resurrection on the south face of its tower. The pleasant white washed interior reveals several signs of Vulliamy's restoration of 1844 (e.g. nave roof), but we especially liked the original parts of the 15th century rood screen and the details in the south arcade capitals.

1. Beverstone Castle

Newington Bagpath
Minute hamlet in a quiet valley overlooked by the circular earthworks (or motte) of a medieval castle, and a small church beside it. We found the church locked, but still enjoyed our visit to its tranquil, overgrown churchyard, with its views out over the valley. The squat tower has an attractively hipped roof, and through the windows we could see a Jacobean pulpit. Apart from this there are old choir stalls and reredos, but little else of interest appears to have survived the restoration of 1858.

2. Newington Bagpath Church

Kingscote
Agreeable village about seven hundred feet above sea level, and well away from the busy main road, on which stands the large virginia creeper covered Hunter's Hall Inn. The manor of Kingscote was held continuously by the Kingscote family from the 12th century until 1956, and one of the family, Catherine, married Doctor Edward Jenner, the discoverer of vaccination, in the church here in 1788. (Don't miss the proud little tablet in the porch proclaiming that ' . . . his marriage brought him much happiness'.) The church has a well proportioned exterior and there are several interesting Kingscote family monuments in the churchyard.

3. Church and Manor, Owlpen

Owlpen
Here is an exquisite group of buildings in a deep hollow beneath woodlands. We first came here in spring, and were enchanted with the manor itself, with the small Victorian church above it, with the clipped yews, the daffodils, and the steep woods acting as a backdrop to it all. The manor dates back to the 15th century and owes something to the 16th, 17th and 18th centuries also. However it is, above all, the Cotswold manor house par excellence . . . a fitting place to end our long series of Cotswold journeys.

4. Owlpen Manor

INDEX

Entry	Page
Alderley	9
Amberley	29
Atkyns, Sir R.	23
Avening	5
Avon Valley	13
Badminton House	7
Bagendon	21
Bagendon Dykes	21
Barnsley Brothers	23
Bathurst, Earl of	23
Baunton	21
Beaufort, Dukes of	7
Belas Knap	17
Beverstone	31
Beverstone Castle	31
Birdlip Hill	15
Bisley	25
Bisley Wells	25
Breakheart Hill	10
Brimpsfield	15
Broad Ride	23
Brockhampton	17
Buckholt Wood	15
Bull's Cross	24
Calcot Cross Roads	30
Caldey Island	15
Calmsden	21
Camber, John	17
Cassey Compton	19
Caudle Green	27
Chantrey, Sir F.	9
Charlton Abbots	17
Chavenage	5
Chedworth	19
Chedworth Roman Villa	19
Chedworth Woods	19
Cherington	5
Churn, River	17
Churn Valley	15, 21
'Cider with Rosie'	25
Cirencester	3
Cirencester Park	3, 23
Cleeve Common	17
Coates	3
Cockleford	15
Colne, River	17, 19
Corinium	3
Cotton, Richard	17
Cowley	15
Cranham Wood	15
Cud Hill	12
Daglingworth	23
Daneway	23
Dowdeswell	17
Drakestone Point	11
Droys Court	15
Dunkirk Cross Roads	8
Duntisbourne Abbots	27
Duntisbourne Leer	27
Duntisbourne Rouse	29
Dursley	11
Eden, F. C.	21, 29
Edge	13, 24
Edgeworth	27
Edward II	15
Elkstone	15
Ermin Street	14, 23
Forest Green	29
Frocester Hill	11
Frome Valley	13, 23, 25, 27
Giant's Cave, The	7
Giffard, John	15
Gimson, E.	23
Golden Valley	13, 25
Great Badminton	7
Hampton Fields	31
Haresfield Beacon	13
Hawkesbury	9
Hazleton Manor	2
Hetty Pegler's Tump	11
Hilcot Brook	17
Hilcot Wood	17
Hillesley	9
Holford, R. S.	7, 31
Horton	9
Horton Court	9
Howe, Sir J.	19
Inchbrook	29
Jenkinson Family	9
Jenner, Dr. E.	31
'John Halifax Gentleman'	29
Kent, William	7
Kilkeney Inn	16
Kingscote	31
Lee, Laurie	25
Little Badminton	7
Long Stone, The	29
Lower Kilcott	9
Luckington	7
Millend	10
Minchinhampton	29
Minchinhampton Common	29
Miserden	27
Morris, William	23
Nag's Head	5
Nailsworth	29
Newark Park	9
Newington Bagpath	31
North Cerney	21
Nympsfield	29
Overley Ride	22
Owlpen	31
Ozleworth	9
Ozleworth Bottom	8
Painswick	25
Painswick Beacon	13
Pinchley Wood	17
Poole, Sir H.	23
Prinknash Abbey	15
Raglan Castle	7
Rendcomb Church	21
Rodborough Common	13
Rodborough Fort	13
Rodmarton	2, 5
Royal Agricultural College	2
Sapperton	23
Scottsquar Hill	12
Selsley Common	10
Sevenhampton	17
Sherston	7
Shipton Oliffe	19
Shipton Solers	19
Shortwood	13
Slad	25
Siimbridge	11
Somerset, General Lord	9
Somerset Monument	9
Starveall Cross Roads	8
Stinchcombe Hill	11
Stockend Woods	12
Stratton	23
Stroud	13
Stroud Musuem	13
Swift's Hill	25
Syde	27
Syreford	18
Tame, Sir E.	21
Tarlton	3
Tetbury	5
Thames Head	3
Thames & Severn Canal	3
Trewsbury Mead	3
Tunley	24, 25
Tunnel House Inn	3
Tyndale, Thomas	21
Uley	11
Uleybury	11
Uley Tumulus	11
Upper Coberley	15
Upper Kilcott	9
Vulliamy, L.	7, 9, 31
Waterlane	24, 25
Waterley Bottom	10
West Down	17
Westonbirt	7
Westonbirt Arboretum	7
Whiteshill	12
White Way, The	21
Whittington	17
Whittington Court	17
Wildfowl Trust, The	11
Windsoredge	29
Winstone	27
Witcombe Roman Villa	15
Witcombe Wood	15
Withington	19
Wontley Farm	17
Woodchester	13
Woodchester Roman Pavement	13
Wortley	8
Wotton-under-Edge	9